Convertible
Dreams

By Patricia Corrigan

**Missouri Center
for the Book**

છે છે છે

Missouri Authors
Collection

Convertible Dreams:
Saturday Morning Musings on Life, Lunch and Matters of the Heart
By Patricia Corrigan

First Edition

ISBN: 1-891442-14-7

Library of Congress Catalog Number: 2001 131630

Publisher's thanks to: Anna Ross, editor; Allison A. Bonvie, inside graphic design; Lisa Pepper, proofreader.

Virginia Publishing Co.
P.O. Box 4538
St. Louis, MO 63108
(314) 367-6612
www.wordnews.com

Table of Contents

ACKNOWLEDGMENTS

Thanks to: David Lipman for assigning me to write the weekly column; every staff member on the *St. Louis Post-Dispatch* features copy desk from 1992 to the present; all my loyal readers; Jeff Fister, Anna Ross and everyone else at Virginia Publishing Co.; Dave Sinclair for letting me sit in a convertible; Nate Warren for taking the photo of me in that car; Joel for not making me change his name to Sam in this book; and kind people everywhere who spent time talking to me and then opened the paper to discover themselves quoted in my column.

*For my son Joel Michael Krauska, who drives
a red convertible and dreams big.*

*And for my Five Favorite Female Friends: Judy Guerrero,
Linda P. Gwyn, Carol North, Beth Remming, Ann Rothery.*

Introduction

So I'm sitting at a stoplight in the heart of St. Louis in my tasteful grown-up-lady car, pondering recent news from my son. After months of research and deliberation, he bought a red convertible. He lives in northern California, and often heads for the shore, just forty-five minutes from his home.

In my mind's eye, I see him driving his shiny new convertible along Highway 1. The Pacific Ocean sparkles in the sun as the car zips along. The air is fresh and clean. The roar of the surf provides background music for the drive.

Then I burst into tears.

That vision of driving a red convertible along Highway 1 is—or was—my dream. Somehow, like the dreams of so many convertible lovers in St. Louis, my dream got downsized to tooling around in our moody, muggy weather in a four-door sedan. That's what happens to many of our dreams, of course. We convert them, we adjust them, we remake them into something that better suits our reality.

That's not all bad. After all, there is something to be said for wanting what you have.

What you have here is a collection of my Saturday morning columns published in the *St. Louis Post-Dispatch* from 1992 through 2000. The book includes your favorites, and mine. Some of the columns address dreams, some deal with reality and one is about a convertible. None of the columns has been changed in any way, and the date of publication appears at the end of each.

I hope the columns make you laugh, make you think or make you look at the world a little differently.

And whatever you drive, I hope you treasure the immense power of dreams.

—*Patricia Corrigan*
Spring 2001

FAVORITE FEMALE FRIENDS

Alas, I have no sisters by birth, but I have spent much of my life developing deep friendships with women I call "sisters of choice," a phrase I swiped from my friend Elizabeth. Nurturing female friendships comes naturally to most women from our earliest days, and we cherish those friendships even more as we age.

A favorite greeting card sums it up nicely: "The circle of women around us weave invisible nets of love that carry us when we're weak and sing with us when we're strong."

This chapter celebrates the circle of women around me.

Ladies Who Lunch

Five of us were out last week playing Ladies Who Lunch.

Four of us work, and the fifth among us is busy too, so it's difficult to find time to be together. But there we were, having lunch on a Thursday afternoon in a Mexican restaurant, celebrating a birthday.

Five other women were seated just across the restaurant from us, and when one of them whooped gleefully, the five of us stopped talking and looked over at their table.

They saw us watching them, and they laughed. Then we all laughed, acknowledging together how much fun it is to be out with women you care about.

The four women I sat at that table with last week are women I have known and loved for more than seventeen years.

When we met, we all were pregnant or caring for infants. We first met at La Leche League meetings, where we went to learn from experienced mothers how to breast-feed our babies.

Through the years, the five of us learned from one another how to be mothers. In the process, we got in the habit of nurturing each other, even as we nurtured our children.

That's what makes our friendship special. None of us lives a remarkable life; yet none of us is ordinary in any way to one another.

Beth and Linda teach school. Judy spends her time organizing fund-raising programs at area schools, volunteering at the Zoo among the animals we both love so much and singing in several choirs. Ann is a self-employed marketing and training consultant.

Each of them has at least one biological sister. I don't, so

I've simply taken on these women as my sisters.

We refer to ourselves as the Five Favorite Female Friends. (Someone once mistook us for the Five Fabulous Females—a name we're considering adopting.)

About once a month, we gather to celebrate a birthday or honor an accomplishment or just to catch up on one another's news.

Together, we have weathered the deaths of several of our parents, one miscarriage, one divorce, assorted cysts, biopsies and minor surgeries, several graduate degrees, job changes (expected and unexpected) and numerous incidents of questionable behavior on the part of our respective husbands and children.

Whenever one of us has needed to talk, the rest of us have listened, both individually and as a group. When the first of us first returned to work, the rest of us offered moral support. When, one by one, four of us had a second child, we took turns cooking and delivering meals to the new mother.

In times of sickness or impending visits from in-laws, we have all pitched in and helped clean the house or do the laundry.

Once, in a gesture above and beyond the call of duty, en masse we emptied, scrubbed out and organized a long-neglected refrigerator.

In the early years, we gathered up our babies and met for lunch at one another's homes. We would sit, talking and drinking pots and pots of herb tea, nibbling on bagels slathered with cream cheese and topped with a slice of fresh tomato.

Some days, we would bundle up the babies and go off to garage sales, or to the Zoo or a neighborhood park.

Now, when our teen-agers are out driving our cars, we bum rides with one another and go to a movie or the theater. Sometimes, we soak in Beth's hot tub. Or we go shopping, and cheerfully advise one another on everything from power suits to couches.

And we do go out to eat together, sitting down to nachos, scampi, gyros, crabmeat salads, gazpacho, vegetarian pizza, chocolate cheesecake or whatever we are in the mood for.

We are friends, and we take great pleasure in sitting down together, talking and taking care of one another.

May all Ladies Who Lunch enjoy such good fortune.

August 1, 1992

Convertible Dreams

Judy's hair is standing on end.

Nothing terrible happened. Quite the contrary—she accidentally bought a Mustang convertible, and now she has "convertible hair," hair tousled by the wind.

Judy set out to replace a well-loved minivan with one of three vehicles: another minivan, a Ford Explorer or a Jeep Cherokee. Her husband and two sons each had a preference, but they agreed to "see what's out there" and then let Judy make the decision.

Judy's friends decided that was silly. We told her she needed a Mustang convertible, and then we found one for her.

Four of us were out one Saturday afternoon, checking out an art show. After the show, we relaxed over a late lunch as Judy told us stories about the horrors of car shopping.

Briefly, she said the model with the air bag looks like a station wagon jacked up on tall wheels. The one that looks good has a bad repair record. As for the minivan—well, Judy's been there and done that. She wasn't sure she wanted another one.

Frankly, she wasn't sure what she wanted.

Then, this: "There was a yellow Mustang convertible in the show room," Judy said, her eyes sparkling for the first time that afternoon.

We decided, en masse, to go see the Mustang.

This is exactly how I came to buy a couch. I scouted out several sofas at different stores, and then I took my Five Favorite Female Friends to sit around on them. We considered the advantages and disadvantages of each, ("Would this look good in a beach house, if I had one?") and I bought a couch.

But I digress.

At the Ford dealer, we got out of the car (a red '91 Oldsmobile Cutlass Supreme) and five salesmen raced over to help us. We didn't want any help, and we said so.

We stopped in the lot to examine the Explorer. As we peered in the windows, we discussed storage of the materials Judy needs for her job. We worried about where to hide packages at Christmas. We rated the upholstery.

Then we went inside to see the Mustang.

Gorgeous!

"Where would I put groceries?" Judy asked. We opened the trunk, which is about the same size as the glove compartment.

"Oh come on! You could put groceries in there," Beth said.

"Short groceries," Linda said.

We admired the car a while longer, and then we left.

Cruising past a Lincoln-Mercury dealership, we saw a used '92 Mustang convertible on the lot. We pulled in just as the last salesman pulled out, so we were able to leisurely inspect the car.

"It's really cute," Judy said.

"This would be really fun," I said.

There was no talk of air bags or repair records or trunk space. Or groceries.

Over dinner that evening, Judy told her father about her day. Before she could elaborate on the advantages and disadvantages of each option, her dad said simply, "Buy the Mustang."

The next morning, a perfect Mustang convertible day if ever there was one, Judy and I took the Mustang out for a test drive.

Riding along, we reminisced about Mustangs in our past (I had a '66, she had a '68) and we talked about how regressing is a positive thing if it makes you feel good.

I felt so good, I went home and dyed my hair red.

Two days later, Judy bought the car and made an appointment to get her hair frosted. The morning she picked up her Mustang convertible, she drove right to my house.

"Let's name her 'Trixie,'" I said as we drove out to Lone Elk Park, a great place to commune with nature from a convertible.

We agreed that we will go for a ride in the convertible every day that the weather is nice.

Honk if you see us—two happy women reliving our pasts, with dyed hair standing on end.

September 18, 1993

Megan Gets Married

Married!

One of the children is to be married, and we mothers all are agog. Megan, the eldest daughter of one of my Five Favorite Female Friends, is the first of our children to make this passage.

We all were startled at the news, but then, the rest of us gave birth mostly to boys who never tell their mothers anything. I do hope to be invited to my son's wedding, should he choose to have one some day, but I suspect I won't hear about it more than a week in advance.

Carol, the mother of the bride-to-be, saw this coming long before the official announcement was made, and she is genuinely pleased.

"If I had picked somebody for her, I couldn't have picked a dearer lad," said Carol. "Don is so sweet—we've known him several years, and we love him."

That said, she added: "The surrealism of it all makes me giggle. I think I'm supposed to be having a nervous breakdown or an anxiety attack, but I'm having neither. I'm giggling."

Then, this: "Something about this event demands a period of time that we are present and, I hope, reflective, in that this is a passage for all of us. Right now, that amuses me. It probably will swat me a good one when it happens."

Probably, it will swat all of us a good one, as we sit there in the pew. After all, if one of the children—Megan is nearly twenty-three—is marrying, can the rest of those babies we nursed and nurtured and then sent off to college be far behind?

Oh, we're coping. We've pooled our money to buy a Significant Gift. We've even tried to figure out what that gift should be. We also have set aside some time to nurture Carol. We've planned a "Pamper Carol" party amid the seven Christmas trees in Linda's lovely home.

There, we'll sit Carol down in the biggest chair, in front of the fire, and bring her a cup of mulled wine. We'll offer her a back rub or a foot massage, or both. We'll listen to her expectations and hopes for the big day, and we'll tell her ours.

Knowing us, we'll also tell each other stories about when the kids were babies. And we'll laugh together, perhaps the best fortification for major events in anyone's life.

Right now, Carol is busier emotionally than physically. Unlike some mothers of brides, Carol is not racing from store to store, picking out printed napkins or gilded matchbooks or floral centerpieces.

Megan and her sister, Emily, have made all the arrangements.

"One by-product of being a working mother is that I have daughters with organizational skills," said Carol. "They've taken care of everything. My role is simply to be the hostess at the party."

Of course, Carol will have to walk down the aisle on cue. No problem. She is an actor and the artistic director of a theater company, so what's one more cue?

"This is very like a performance," she said, "except you don't do it twice." She sighed. "My hope is that I can just be present, and let the event happen."

Right.

Carol is the kind of person who weeps while watching Hallmark card commercials.

Giggling again, Carol admitted that is true.

"I want to feel it all intensely, but I'm afraid of just that. This is a very public thing. Will I have the elan to be a grown-up?"

Of course she will, as will we all.

As I write this, all these events—the wedding, the party for Carol—are still in the future. By the time you read this, Carol will have been pampered and Megan and Don will have been married.

Here's a wish for a happy new life together for them. And a Happy New Year for the rest of us.

December 31, 1994

Emily Has a Baby

No small issues were on the agenda one evening last week. No, we grappled with the biggies, Birth and Death and Staying and Leaving. It was a night for tears of joy, tears of sorrow and tears of recognition, all spilled in the company of close friends.

Carol gets credit for the first part of the evening. Carol is one of my Five Favorite Female Friends, women I met when we all were nursing our babies more than twenty years ago. These women remain my closest friends, and are my "sisters of choice," siblings who unaccountably were born into five different families.

Carol's daughter Emily just gave birth to the beautiful Anna Elizabeth, the first child born to any of our eleven offspring. We surrogate grandmothers, all proud as proud can be, gathered at Carol's home a week ago to watch the video of the baby's first twenty-four hours. Within seconds after the tape began to play, there was much cooing and whimpering and clucking.

Not on the part of the baby—these sounds all rose unbidden from us, as we watched a young woman we've known for all her twenty-three years cuddle her firstborn. We sighed happily when Glen, Anna's father, held the baby close. We grinned knowingly at one another when Emily showed Anna her room. And we gasped in unison when the baby sneezed. Then we laughed, at ourselves and for joy, even as we wiped away tears.

The next videotape that Carol shared with us was a program featured on *Nightline* last Christmas. "The Gift: The Power of Music at the Threshold Between Life and Death" is about a project called The Chalice of Repose. Carol has the tape because her sister Jocelyn works with the project.

Jocelyn is a certified musical thanatologist, a person trained to help ease the physical pain and mental distress of the dying by accompanying the transition from this world to the next with gentle harp music and quiet melodic chants. To date, she has participated in more than 180 of these "musical vigils" in hospitals, hospices and homes.

Therese Schroeder-Sheker, a native of Des Plaines, Illinois, founded the project, which has operated out of St. Patrick Hospital in Missoula, Montana, for the past five years. A concert performer, recording artist and medieval music scholar, she developed the two-year certification program that allows musical thanatologists to be part of the medical teams that provide palliative care to people at the end of their lives.

Schroeder-Sheker gives credit to Benedictine monks living in the eleventh century in southern France for first using soft music free of rhythm, pulse or count to assist "a blessed death." Her first experience came twenty-five years ago, while working as an aide in a nursing home. There, on impulse, she sang softly one evening to a man in his last moments, holding him and literally serving as a midwife to his dying. "That man reached out a few inches and pointed the way to my future," she said on the show.

Doctors who once were skeptical gave testimony about patients whose heart rates and breathing slowed during the musical vigils held by Schroeder-Sheker and her students. In a particularly poignant segment, a forty-eight-year-old judge close to death said, "Their music provides a place for me to accept my death. Sometimes, I cry. Sometimes, I sleep. Sometimes, I do both." The man's daughter said that she could not give her father "the words of comfort that this music can" and that her own fears had been "washed away" by the music.

This profoundly moving program drew us all in, bringing forth tears for both the beauty of the project and the people whose lives were ending even as we watched. We laughed only when Ann broke the silence by saying, "OK, do that for me when I'm dying. I want to sign up."

We all were "signed up" that same evening to see Anthony Clarvoe's *Ambition Facing West* at the Repertory Theatre, a powerful play about four generations of family members taking turns leaving home to avoid staying and staying home to avoid leaving. More than one character in the play points out that it's all the same in the end, that what really matters will circle back to us farther up the path, usually when we least expect it.

So, too, I think, it is with birth and death. They are not unrelated events, but part of the same cycle that includes many decisions to leave and decisions to stay. As Schroeder-Sheker says on the videotape, people do die, but the experience can plant in all of us seeds of hope—not unlike the seeds of hope that come with the birth of Anna Elizabeth.

October 25, 1997

Party Preparations

Down in the basement, rooting through mementos from my past, I discovered questions about the past, the present and the future.

In retrospect, I wish I had anticipated the laughter, the tears and the temporary identity crisis that resulted from that hour sifting through boxes. I would have done it anyway, but now you're forewarned, just in case you're inclined to run downstairs and look through the souvenirs of your life.

A party invitation sent me on this journey. My Five Favorite Friends, women I've spent quality time with for more than twenty years, routinely acknowledge one another's birthdays.

In this case, we're celebrating two at once, Beth's and Carol's. Usually, we go to dinner or a movie or just gather at one of our homes for an evening together.

This party will be different. The invitation, issued by Carol and Beth, reads, "Please bring no food or presents. Instead, we ask you to bring another kind of gift . . . a significant piece of your past that you have not previously shared with the rest of us."

Beth and Carol asked that we bring an artifact—or a placeholder for the real thing—that somehow "holds the piece of your past that you want to share."

We're instructed to bring the artifact inside a box, bag or container that will conceal it "until we open our gifts, these stories-not-yet-told to each other."

This change in how we celebrate birthdays is due in part to Carol's search for significance in relationships, something beyond the comfortable camaraderie the six of us share. Beth, whose birthday falls shortly after Carol's, eagerly embraced Carol's suggestions, and we set a date.

First reactions to the invitation were varied.

"I have no secrets," said Linda. "I can't think of anything to bring."

"I know exactly what I'm bringing," said Ann.

"I have nothing to bring, because I lost a lot in the fire," said Judy.

"I have plenty of things I could bring, and they all are in the basement," I said.

Of course, I know what's in those boxes. Maybe I don't recall every letter, every photo, every diary entry, but I haven't lost touch with the girl who saved them all. You probably know what you've stashed away as well, even if just in a general way. But mental sifting wasn't going to help me complete the assignment, so one evening after work, I headed for the storage closet in the basement.

Among my treasures, I found my brother's Little League glove, two character dolls from Mexico, a Davy Crockett mug, a lace handkerchief from an Irish pen pal, pictures from my sixth birthday party, a maraca with "Cuba" etched on the side, a painted plaster cocker spaniel with rhinestone eyes and stacks of letters from my friend Susan.

In another box, I found five diaries full of earnest entries, including one that noted confidently that a boy I liked had accepted three cough drops from me in the course of a single day, surely proof that he liked me. In a bag of my baby clothes, I ran across the dress I wore as a flower girl in Jackie and George Maloney's wedding when I was three. In the same bag, I also unearthed my first pair of Mary Janes, scuffed white leather shoes that I wore as a toddler, the same style of shoe I prefer today.

In a tiny box, I discovered tiny toys. After opening a doll's trunk, I carefully handled the clothes that my mother made for my doll Pat, who walked if you helped her. Today, Pat's eyes are rolled back in her head, rather like Linda Blair's in that awful movie, but her wardrobe remains exquisite, a collection that includes a gabardine coat with a fur collar, a rose-colored satin evening gown and denim overalls and a flannel shirt. In another box, I found my doll Ellen. Her rubber arms are cracked and sunken, but the face on her hard-plastic head gazed at me sweetly, and I inexplicably slipped her yellow knit cap over her bare head to help keep her warm in the chilly basement.

As I sat amidst tangible evidence of the girl I was, I wondered for a bit about who I am now and who I hope to be in the future. I very nearly wrote there "when I grow up," but as I'm approaching fifty, maybe I need to start thinking of myself as a grown-up. After all, I now eat mushrooms.

The answers to those questions, whatever they may be, did not address which memento, which part of my past, to take to the party.

Perhaps I need to bundle up Pat and Ellen and even Angel with her broken shoulder and present my friends with these old friends who once dressed so well. Or maybe I should consider taking some of those diaries.

As I write this, I have forty-eight hours left to decide. I'll let you know, because I suspect this particular birthday party will be well worth writing about. Watch this space.

February 7, 1998

Post-Party Mortem

Two weeks ago, I wrote here about an invitation to a birthday party that required guests to bring "a significant piece of your past that you have not previously shared with the rest of us." That was quite a challenge, as the guests at this party were my Five Favorite Female Friends, women I've spent quality time with for more than twenty years.

The assignment sent me scurrying to the storage closet in the basement, to sort through the boxes marked "Pat's Past." I wrote here about the sorting, about the laughter, the tears and the temporary identity crisis that resulted from that hour sifting through boxes. Some of you wrote or called to say you had been on similar journeys recently, and other readers called to ask what I took to the party.

People. I took people to the party, people who had pestered me about going from the moment the invitation arrived. Specifically, I took my mother, my father and my brother. None of them are living—Daddy died in 1982, Mom in 1973 and my brother in 1963—so I had to make do with artifacts from their lives.

"Every day, all day, I am part of a family that no one can see," I told my friends that evening. "I've brought some items to help you get to know Bonnie Corrigan, Joseph Timothy William Patrick Corrigan and Mike Corrigan."

My brother suffered from kidney disease five of the ten years he lived. Still, my parents provided as normal a life as possible for all of us, and one of Mike's passions was his Cub Scout softball team. I took his team trophy from 1962, and also a picture of us with Santa taken a few years earlier.

When Mom died suddenly, she was making big plans for her retirement, plans to attend college and plans to spend quality time with any grandchildren I might produce. I took something to the party that reflected her earlier years—a fire engine-red taffeta dress that she wore in local dance competitions long before marriage and motherhood. Her dance partner was a male friend who gave her an opal ring before he died in World War II. I have that ring and also the sassy dress, which has a flared skirt and a bolero jacket.

A small molded-plastic jewelry box with an Asian motif sat on Daddy's dresser for as long as I can remember, and I took that to the party. The tiny drawers house an odd collection that includes mine and Mike's beaded baby bracelets, receipts for money Daddy sent home while serving in World War II, and assorted safe-driving pins he later earned while driving a beer truck for Anheuser-Busch.

None of these artifacts fully represents the people who owned them, of course. My goal was simply to introduce my family members. They may be gone, but to my mind, they live in me, through my memories, through beliefs and personality quirks that I inherited from them and through the profound sense of connection I feel with them.

Carol brought a bedroll, a symbol of happy times spent with her father, who died in 1994. In her youth, the two of them regularly attended a summer camp, Carol as a camper and her father as a counselor. During the last days of his life, Carol and the members of her family stayed by his bedside, and Carol talked with him about their many adventures. At the party, we sang a song popular at the camp, which Carol led in her father's honor.

Ann presented us with her 4-H study guide on floral arrangements, a souvenir from time spent during her youth as a Milo Merry Maiden in Milo, Illinois. The book included guidelines for floral arrangements for homes, churches and public buildings, and Ann's sketches provided a surprising peek into her past.

In high school, Judy spent a summer traveling the world with her parents and her sister. She brought a bracelet brimming with sterling silver charms collected in each country and assorted travel stories.

Beth produced her Phi Beta Kappa key "that proves I'm smart" and an artificial flower representative of when she was named Kappa Alpha Rose by a fraternity on her campus, "which proves I'm pretty." Beth also showed us two awards she has won recently as a teacher, tangible evidence that she is good at what she does.

Linda passed around the engine and the first car of her toy train, a symbol from her childhood that has influenced her standards for herself and others ever since. When they gave her the train, Linda's parents assured her it was "the finest quality." Linda said she still tries to fill her life with the best, be it toys or relationships or everything in between.

In the course of the evening, we laughed, we cried, we ate lots of rye chips. We learned more about one another as we heard stories from our respective pasts and gained insight into our present lives, as well. All told, it was an evening of the finest quality.

February 21, 1998

The Other Patricia Corrigan

This message came via e-mail late in April, from one Agnes Puff: "Would you believe I received a phone call Saturday evening for you from *People* magazine? He said he would like to interview you for an article about single women. I hope you do the interview and let me know when it will appear in *People*. I'll be sure to get a copy."

The fact that *People* magazine was looking for me is interesting but not nearly as interesting as the true identity of Agnes Puff.

That is the e-mail name of Patricia Corrigan. The Other

Patricia Corrigan. The one that had my name before I did but gets hassled with phone calls and mail for me because my name—our name—appears in the newspaper regularly. Here's what happens: People from out of town (such as the people from *People* and other people who don't know me well) try to reach me by looking me up in the phone directory or calling directory assistance. I'm not listed, but The Other Patricia Corrigan is.

TOPC received sympathy cards when my father died. A friend of a friend sent her a large-size lingerie catalog meant for me. Once, TOPC was invited to a Halloween party by people she did not know. She figured they knew me, and she called them to explain the mix-up. My friends, good people one and all, invited her to come to the party anyway. As I recall, neither of us was able to make it. Another evening, I showed up at Gitto's on The Hill with four female friends for a birthday dinner. The host at the restaurant was all in a dither, certain that there must be a mistake on the reservations list because TOPC had just left with four of her Favorite Female Friends.

I first learned about TOPC shortly after I started working for the *Post-Dispatch* some eighteen years ago. One Monday morning at the office, columnist Elaine Viets told me she had tried to call me over the weekend to encourage me to attend a union meeting. She had called the Patricia Corrigan in the phone book. Apparently, they had a lovely chat, and TOPC told Elaine she surely hoped I would go to the meeting. And I did. Once or twice, I got calls at work from people who had been referred by TOPC. Today, my telephone number, address, fax number and e-mail address all appear in the paper three times a week, so most people have no trouble finding me at the office.

Well, except the people from *People*. I did return that call, and as soon as the reporter found out I have not been single my entire life, he lost interest in interviewing me. That's fame—easy come, easy go.

The end of May, I got a much more important e-mail from TOPC. "I received a commencement announcement in the mail which I think is for you," she wrote. "It is from a young woman named Christa and a senior picture is included with it. It is quite a good picture. I thought you might like to have it." I did indeed want that announcement and photo, and we exchanged e-mails to figure out how to make that happen. (I also called Christa's mother and teased her about addressing envelopes incorrectly. Her defense was that both Patricia Corrigans live on streets with French names and we have the same ZIP code. She's right.)

In the course of our e-mails, I asked TOPC how she chose the e-mail name of Agnes Puff. Here is what she said: "Any time I went to a card party and put my name on the ticket for an attendance prize, I would NEVER win. I thought I would fool the gods and I put down 'Agnes.' Guess what? I won! Puff was my kitty that I had for many years. So in this way I keep her memory alive."

After reading that, I thought how much I wanted to meet TOPC. I have numerous aliases, and I love cats. I figured we would get along. We had lunch one day in June, and we had a wonderful time. TOPC used to work for the telephone company, and now she is retired. Her middle name is "Ann," just like mine, and we both live in condos in Creve Coeur. She likes to eat out, and so do I. We both drive 1998 Oldsmobiles. We both have been to Ireland, where we felt right at home among all those people who look so much like us, though neither of us tried to track down relatives there. Because neither of us knows much in the way of detailed family history, we aren't even sure whether we are cousins.

"So," I said at one point during lunch (we both had the crab cakes), "how much hassle is it with people confusing us? Does it happen often?" TOPC said it really isn't all that often. Still, sometimes in a department store, if she writes a check, someone will ask her if she writes for the *Post-Dispatch*.

"I tell them I do," she said, eyes twinkling. I laughed. I understand completely. There was a time, usually in elevators, when people would learn that I worked at the paper and then they would ask what my byline was. I always said I was Elaine Viets.

Anyway, TOPC and I are not the same person, though we now are friends. If you want to reach her, look her up in the phone book. If you're looking for me, check out my column in the *St. Louis Post-Dispatch*.

July 15, 2000

TURKEY MATH AND MONEY MADNESS

Regular readers know I am mathematically retarded. I don't understand numbers and, more importantly, numbers don't understand me. Because money is generally considered in numerical terms, managing money also is a huge challenge for me. (Finding money to manage is another problem, but I think that's related to shoe shopping, not math.)

Anyway, in this chapter, I wrestle with math and money matters.

Usually, of course, I lose.

Hyacinths for the Soul

Some local stores have posted signs in their windows that read: "Say Buy to the Recesssion." Granted, popularly accepted economic theories usually confuse me. But this looks like a trap.

We should all rush out and buy things we don't need with money we don't have so times will get better?

Maybe that will end the recession and maybe it won't. Maybe it will help out the shop owners who post the signs. Maybe it won't. But without a doubt, such behavior will jack up those credit card bills and we'll all be stuck with more knickknacks to dust.

Besides, if we spend money because that sign tells us to, aren't we embracing George Herbert Bush's questionable theory that we are to blame for the rotten economy?

I knew this country was in trouble long before Bush abandoned the phrase "economic downturn" in favor of "recession." I knew because I gave up recreational shopping. I quit cold turkey (OK, room-temperature turkey) with the help of a new philosophy.

I no longer tell myself that I can't shop or I mustn't shop or I don't need to shop. I had always countered those arguments with "Shut up. I WANT to shop."

And then I would go buy things I didn't need with money I didn't have.

Now, I tell myself "I already have everything I want." It works. You don't have to learn twelve steps to master it. There is just the one phrase: "I have everything I want."

Not that I save money. I don't believe in that.

I don't save money because I don't believe in the future. I

learned this from my family, all of whom died before they meant to and before they had a chance to spend money they had been saving. (Lest you're having visions of a wealthy, fun-loving orphan, forget it. I promptly spent the modest sum they left behind.)

Certainly, it's OK to save a little money over a short period of time, to spend on specific items, such as airline tickets and champagne. But there doesn't seem much point, as I see it, to saving money for the future.

Live now, I say.

Just do it, Nike urges.

Jam today, Lewis Carroll wrote.

Although I no longer believe in spending money on stuff for myself, I do still believe in helping other people accumulate more knickknacks to dust. This generosity of spirit is also espoused by one Jeffrey Blum, a psychologist who lives in Connecticut.

Writing in *Atlantic Monthly* some twelve years ago, Blum said: "Actually, saving money is not in my repertoire of behaviors. I give gifts, for example, as if every day were Christmas."

Blum went on to list in detail all the delicious occasions on which he gives gifts, including, "I like to give gifts to people who come to visit me, but I worry about embarrassing them if they haven't brought anything."

After reading that article, I immediately wanted to run out and buy Blum a lovely gift—something from Tiffany's, for instance. Instead, I wrote to him, and he wrote back, and he later wrote a wonderful book called *Living With Spirit in a Material World* about how stuff is not the answer, but that's another story.

Maybe you already say "buy" to the recession. Maybe you save your money in a sock under your mattress. Maybe you play the stock market or penny-a-point poker or the lottery.

Whatever your financial planning strategy, here is some sound advice, masquerading in the form of an allegedly ancient Chinese proverb:

"If you have but three coins, buy bread with one, give one to the poor and spend one on hyacinths for the soul."

Perhaps if purchasing hyacinths for the soul—any little, lovely treat for you or me or a good friend or even Jeffrey Blum—will boost the economy, then maybe we should "Say Buy to the Recession."

February 1, 1992

Math Anxiety

Go figure—a researcher in Tucson rounded up a roomful of five-month-old infants to determine whether they can add and subtract small numbers of objects mentally.

Karen Wynn, an assistant professor of psychology at the University of Arizona, showed sixteen babies rubber Mickey Mouse dolls, adding and then taking away some of the dolls as she recorded how much time the babies spent gazing at the display area.

Scientists say Wynn's studies prove that babies tend to look longer at things that are new or unexpected, and that conclusion suggests that the ability to grasp the rudiments of arithmetic is inborn.

I say that Wynn has stumbled onto the cause of math anxiety—strangers who take your dolls away.

Maybe Wynn is one of those people who played the violin at two, competed in gymnastics at five and ran her own day-care center at seven, and therefore has no problem asking infants to do math. Or maybe she has tender, moving memories from her own productive days spent in the crib and wants to enhance the self-esteem of babies who only thought they were happy grinning and kicking at the mobiles hanging above their heads.

In any case, Wynn sticks by her findings.

"This study shows a fundamental aspect of cognition," Wynn said in a telephone interview. "The better we understand how the normal mind works, the better we can understand how the abnormal mind works."

Not that she's calling babies born without the math gene "abnormal." In fact, Wynn said her studies cannot predict which babies will be whizzes at math later in life and which will need constant reassurance that one plus one equals two.

I'm in the latter group.

Now it can be told—I am mathematically retarded.

Numbers give me headaches and make me cry. My eyes glaze over at the sight of numbers so big they need commas to separate them. And I forget little numbers, such as my age or how much I have in my savings account. Probably there is a twelve-step program somewhere that could help me, but as I am only comfortable dealing with numbers divisible by five, I wouldn't be able to participate.

(I do know how to figure out tips, because my mother taught me a math secret. You take 10 percent of the bill and double that. If you've had good service, you leave the 20 percent tip. If you've had only so-so service, you put some of the money back in your purse.)

A friend once tried to cure my math anxiety. Mark Driscoll, a very nice man with a graduate degree in differential geometry (whatever that is), decided to set my mind at ease by explaining mathematics to me in a caring, non-threatening way.

No thanks, I said. I'm happy just the way I am. If God had meant for me to understand numbers, She wouldn't have invented calculators, I said.

Fortunately, I have found my niche in life—a newsroom. At work, I am surrounded by talented, intelligent people who are no better at math than I am.

At one time, you could get a journalism degree at most universities without taking any math classes. All of us who had wrestled with sums and theorems and parallelepipeds all through high school promptly and gleefully enrolled in journalism programs.

Now we all work together, nurturing one another through monthly checkbook statements, offering moral support to reporters working on budget issues and suffering mightily together when somebody needs help figuring a percentage for a story on property tax assessments.

We may never know how many of us suffer today because we fell into the hands of researchers who tried to teach us math in our early years by taking away our dolls.

September 5, 1992

Creative Accounting

My bank was just swallowed up by another bank.

This is the third time an establishment where I chose to keep my money has been taken over by an establishment where I chose not to keep my money.

Every time a huge bank absorbs a smaller bank or a savings and loan, the huge bank raises all the fees and drives away customers like me who see no reason to give lots of money to a bank just for the privilege of doing business there. Today, there are fewer banks that don't charge customers astronomical fees. Also, there are fewer banks willing to work with me once they hear about my personal accounting system.

Basically, I hide money from myself in my checking account. I've developed three clever ways to hide money in an account:

First, keep a wad of money on deposit that never appears on the check register. I squirrel away $100, because my bank charges a monthly fee if the account drops any lower.

Keeping the minimum amount on hand provides a safety cushion, a margin for error, and keeping it out of sight—off the check register—keeps it out of mind.

Usually.

Second, ignore the exact amount of cents on any check you write.

I started this because it required too much math to figure out a handful of change. I always record the exact amount of any checks I write, but when I calculate my balance, I round up or down, depending on whether the figure is over fifty cents or under fifty cents. That way, I always have a few dollars more than I think I do.

My third hint for successful account management is somewhat complicated.

In the check register, I have several amounts entered in parentheses. That's money I need to cover specific anticipated expenses. For instance, every year in November when I collect my Christmas Club earnings, I immediately deposit the check in my account, but I put the figure in parentheses.

Unlike some Christmas Club members who actually spend their funds on making a joyous holiday for loved ones, I use the money to pay my property taxes. I learned the hard way one year that it is not easy to suddenly gather up $800 from my petty cash (that's $10 in the cookie jar). I decided the Christmas Club was a relatively painless way to save that money.

Anyway, my rule is that all special funds may be deposited, but not calculated into the balance until the bill is due. Otherwise, the money set aside for specific purposes migrates into the money set aside for general purposes, and soon there is no money for any purpose whatsoever.

That's my system—you just lie to yourself at all times about how much money you have, but you lie on the side of extra cash.

There are some drawbacks to this system.

For one thing, you never know exactly how much money you have. When the bank statement comes, and you sit down to balance the account, you have to remember how to deal with money in parentheses and you have to remember that you are hiding $100 or $300 or whatever your minimum deposit is.

On just three occasions over the last ten years, I've gone to the bank for help so I could figure out exactly where I stood. Once, a patient woman at the bank figured it all out for me. At another appointment, the bank officer laughed throughout my explanation of my system. Last month, the woman I spoke with suggested I consider closing the account so the bank could give me an accurate figure once and for all. Then I could start over with a new account.

Now that I'm getting a new bank foisted on me, that's exactly what I'll do. Somewhere else.

September 4, 1993

Easy Come, Easy Go

Has the economy crashed?

A couple of weeks ago, I paid off all my credit card bills

(AGAIN) and then I left the country. I'm back, and I want to apologize if I caused an upset in the already questionable financial health of the nation.

Just before I ran away, I read that consumer credit had soared in April, the eleventh straight monthly increase. Apparently credit card borrowing set a record, with an increase of nearly $5 billion, pushing the grand total up to $293.8 billion.

I don't care to name the actual numbers I owed, but I can say that the amount was a mere pittance of that $293.8 billion. Still, it was no pittance to me.

Here's what happened: I got a modest check in the mail for some free-lance writing. By modest, I mean much more than usual but not as much as high-profile writers get. It was nowhere near the $24 million that a local couple won in the Missouri Lottery two weeks ago, but the figure on the check did have a comma in it, unlike my weekly paycheck. That is to say—well, we're talking $11,000.

The money arrived on a Thursday. After dancing around the living room in a fit of giggles, I dashed off to the bank. The teller told me that I couldn't use the money for three business days.

"This check will clear at midnight on Monday," she said.

I made plans to stay up late Monday and go on a spending spree. Then I went home and wrote a bunch of checks—dated for Tuesday, of course.

First things first—and first, I signed up for ten therapeutic massages. You get a $100 discount if you pay for ten at one time. I sent a small donation to a whale conservation organization. And I ordered an arcane journal published by my friend Ricky Jay. The water bill was due. I paid it. I sent off to a catalog company for a T-shirt for my son. The shirt reads "Theater is life. Film is art. Television is furniture."

Then I wrote a check for $1,800, to pay for a plane that I

inadvertently chartered in Mexico in March.

Warming up to big spending, I paid in full the balance on three credit card accounts. Those cards were cluttered with charges for assorted plane tickets, the occasional bottle of good wine and—oh yes—a couch.

I made a payment on the home improvement loan. And I signed a check to Union Electric for a bill that wasn't even due. I tidied up a few more expenses, gleefully writing "PAID IN FULL" on the receipts. Then I left the house to do some grocery shopping.

When I got back home, I sat down to balance the checkbook. I discovered that in the course of the afternoon, I had whipped through $10,000! What was left in the account was earmarked for a vacation. If I spent it, I would have to stay home. Why is it that when I am nouveau riche, it's never for very long? I succumbed to a little Irish melancholy.

What about my hot tub? I fantasize daily about owning a hot tub.

Two hours after I deposited what had seemed like lots of money, and four days before the money was even available to me, I was back to my usual life on the edge—or at least the edge as I know it. Sliding ever deeper into despair, suddenly I remembered my favorite line from the movie *Bugsy*.

When Bugsy Siegel is told that construction of his hotel in Las Vegas cannot proceed because he is out of money, Warren Beatty, in the title role, grins and says:

"Money is just dirty paper with words printed on it, and I can always get some more."

July 9, 1994

Turkey Math

OK, so I mislaid the brand-new turkey lifter, and we had to struggle as usual with assorted spatulas, meat forks and pancake turners. Nonetheless, we got the turkey lifted in good time from the roasting pan to the cookie sheet and then onto the biggest platter in the house. Maybe the turkey lifter will show up in time for Christmas, but regardless, Thanksgiving at my place was a huge hit.

The biggest challenge every Thanksgiving and Christmas, even bigger than successfully lifting the turkey without an implement designed to do just that, is Turkey Math, a requirement if you're planning to cook a bird. Turkey Math, of course, refers to figuring out just how long the bird must cook.

Here's how it always goes at my house:

Let's see, if the turkey cost $16 and crosses the road at a speed of—no, wait, it was a chicken that crossed the road, so there's no need to figure out the speed. OK, if the turkey costs $16 and weighs 20 pounds—no, wait, that's backwards. The turkey costs $20 and weighs 16 pounds and a little bit.

Better get the exact number.

Well, the box the turkey came in says it weighs 16 pounds, 8 ounces. OK, take 16.8 and multiply by 20 minutes. That's 336 minutes, so divided by 60, you get 5.6 hours. Unless, of course, you follow that other Rule of Turkey Cooking, which favors cooking the bird 15 minutes for each pound. OK, 16.8 times 15 minutes is 252 minutes, or 4.2 hours.

Hold everything!

On the bag the bird is wrapped in, it says the turkey weighs 16 pounds, 4 ounces. Well, 16.4 times 15 minutes is

246 minutes, or 4.1 hours. If you figure 16.4 times 20 minutes, you get 328 minutes, which is 5.4666666 hours. So—now we have to decide whether to cook the turkey 4.1 hours or 5.6 hours or something in between that involves way too many sixes.

I'm getting a headache. Can we order a pizza instead?

No. We're going to get this right.

I like numbers with fives in them, so usually, I round the bird's weight up or down to include a five. In this case, that would be 16.5, which is a nice compromise between the weight listed on the bag and the weight listed on the box. Never mind that 16.5 clearly has nothing to do with the real weight of the turkey; just trust me.

Now, if we go with 20 minutes per pound, we're looking at 330 minutes, or a tidy 5.5 hours. If we try 15 minutes per pound, we get 247.5 minutes, or 4.125 hours. Clearly, the only fair thing to do here is cook the turkey for 4 hours and 45 minutes and hope for the best.

Good, that's settled.

The second-biggest challenge during the holidays is finding ginger preserved in syrup for cranberry-ginger conserve, my signature cranberry dish.

We're not talking crystallized ginger or fresh ginger root or preserves of any sort, but actual ginger, candied, and packed in syrup. Ordinarily, the Cheese Place carries it, but this year, they were out of it just before Thanksgiving. They offered to order it, and promised it would be in sometime in December, so I was set for Christmas. Luckily, I discovered that Starr's on Big Bend now carries it, so I was able to make my cranberry-ginger conserve for Thanksgiving, too.

I ripped the recipe out of *The New York Times Magazine* so long ago that the clipping is yellowed, but the actual cranberry-ginger conserve is easy, elegant and delicious.

Here's how to make it:

CRANBERRY-GINGER CONSERVE
1 cup white wine
1 cup granulated sugar
1 (12-ounce) bag cranberries, rinsed
Grated rind of one large lemon
1/2 cup golden raisins
1/2 cup ginger preserved in syrup, finely chopped, and 2 to 3 tablespoons of the syrup

In a stainless-steel or enamel saucepan, mix the wine and sugar with 1/2 cup water. Bring to a boil.

Add the cranberries. Cover and simmer for about 5 minutes, until the berries pop open. Add the lemon rind, raisins, ginger and syrup. Simmer 2 to 3 minutes. Remove from heat and let cool.

Refrigerate overnight before serving.

Yield: About 6 cups.

You can dish up cranberry-ginger conserve with turkey, ham, chicken or pork and know you're doing the main course a big favor. For that matter, you can drizzle it over ice cream and call it dessert, too, as the not-quite-sweet, not-quite-tangy flavor is most adaptable.

And—this is the real bonus—you do not need any special implements to lift cranberry-ginger conserve out of the dish and onto the plate. A simple spoon will do nicely.

Enjoy!

December 6, 1997

401K Madness

Just to irk my friend Carl, I would say all the time that I was going to dump my 401K and run away to Greece or buy fine wines or even pay the electric bill.

"Oh, right," he'd say, smirking. "That's a great idea. Maybe I'll take mine out, too."

Up until last week, I still believed that it was possible to claim your 401K, to cash it all in and roll around in it. I knew you had to wait until you were $59^{1/2}$. I still remember being hacked off when, at age thirty-five, I first found out I had a long wait before I'd see any of this money. I stomped right off to the employee benefits office, and begged them to tell me it wasn't true. It's true, they said. Don't even think about touching that money until you are $59^{1/2}$, or serious penalties will apply.

I cultivated patience. I continued to grow older. Last week, I realized I'll be $59^{1/2}$ in just about $8^{1/2}$ years. I raced around the house, looking for a calendar that extended that far, so I could schedule a 401K retrieval party and invite everybody over on the day that I pick up my money. A gabby sort, I started bragging to friends just how soon the money will be mine.

"You don't want to spend it," said Jerry. "You'll want to live on the interest."

"Oh, you can't actually have the 401K money," said Edward. "You'll need it to support you in your retirement."

"That money is there for later," said Jim. "The last thing you will want to do when you turn $59^{1/2}$ is get the money out and spend it."

I'm outraged. I'm appalled. I'm depressed. I finally learned the value of putting away money now for then, and now I find out that even when then comes, I can't have my own money.

"You don't understand," I said to Jim. "My son just got his first job, and he'll be making $20,000 more a year than I make. Joel will never need my money, so I get to spend it."

A long-suffering look crossed Jim's usually patient face. "It's only OK to spend your 401K money if you know exactly what day you're going to die," he said. "If you guess wrong and you're out of money before you're dead, you'll end up living in a one-room apartment somewhere, eating cat food."

No wonder I'm depressed.

Jim covers money and banking for the *Post-Dispatch*. We sit next to each other. Because of his good influence, I now have a modest "safety net" fund. In all innocence, I confided one day a few years ago that I didn't have a savings account. Jim asked me about a safety net.

"I guess I've always thought of my dad as my safety net," I said.

"And when did he die?" Jim asked.

"In 1982."

"Are you saying you have some money left from his estate?"

"Oh, no. I used what he left me to help send Joel to college," I said.

Jim was outraged, appalled and depressed, and then bullied me into setting aside a little "just in case" money. Truth be told, I had come to consider my credit union as my safety net. When the furnace went out, I called the credit union. "Tell me what you need and I'll get the paperwork right to you," the loan officer said. Now, that's a safety net. Of course, I knew the credit union would expect to get the money back.

Jim was under the impression that if my furnace went out, I should have money set aside to pay for such emergencies. I've never been able to think like that, which is why I panic every time Jim suggests that we switch jobs. "You could write columns telling readers how to spend every penny they have," he says now and then. There are a couple of problems with this idea. Probably, I don't need to elaborate here on my lack of expertise on money and banking, but you do need to know that Jim's idea of a great lunch is a can of soup heated up in the office kitchen, so he's not qualified to do my job, either.

But back to the matter at hand. All these years, I've been holding my breath hoping Joel would be launched in a career and prove able to support himself. Bingo—that has happened. I was so certain that now, my 401K money truly could be mine.

"I'm determined to spend at least some of the principal," I said to Jim. "Can't I at least pay off the condo?"

"No," he said. "The interest you'll earn off the principal will be more than a monthly payment on the condo. You need to put the 401K money where it can work for you so you have money throughout your retirement."

I didn't have the nerve to ask about buying emerald earrings. Clearly, all this money I've been putting away every week is going to end up in Joel's bank account, and he won't even need it.

I need it. More importantly, I want it. And now everybody tells me I can't have it. What a scam!

Just in case you didn't know the ugly truth, I am writing this column as a public service.

May 1, 1999

Financial Advice

Plagued by questions about retirement, well aware that then is suddenly a lot closer to now than it used to be, I sought advice from financial advisers. Greg and Eric are really nice guys, smart and talented, but already I wonder how long this relationship will last. Read on, and you'll see why.

At our first meeting, I turned over all my financial records, which included a questionnaire they had asked me to fill out. At our second visit, they answered my questions about the mortgage and retirement. (Yes, I must continue to make the mortgage payments and no, I won't have enough money to retire at sixty. Or even sixty-two. Or maybe any time before I'm dead.) Next, Eric and Greg noted that I have an extra $1,100 at the end of each month.

An extra $1,100 a month? I'd like to report a theft.

I asked where they got that absurd figure. They got it, of course, from the list of monthly expenses that I turned in. I laughed. Those numbers weren't necessarily correct. I took the questionnaire seriously, of course, but as soon as I handed it over, I remembered additional expenses for some categories and realized I'd estimated too high on other categories.

Do you know offhand how much money you spend each month on your pets? Neither did I, so I estimated how much food the cats eat each year and added in the cost of annual shots at the vet. I neglected to take into consideration my "peace of mind" visits when I need to hear that Ginger, now thirteen, still appears to be healthy. Entertainment also was a tricky category. I added up the cost of theater tickets, assorted concerts and the occasional movie, but I was stuck when it came to books. Are books considered entertainment or education?

Maybe I should have listed books under the "gifts" category. On the other hand, maybe that category just means gifts for other people. Where, then, do I list the goodies that are part of my Pamper Pat Program? In any case, I'm sure I underestimated how much I spend on gifts. I know this because last weekend, I bought enough gifts—mostly for other people—to eat up three months in that category alone.

Then there is the "vacation" category. Three years ago, I charged a trip to Egypt. The trip was not a mistake, but the method of payment was. Eventually, I did pay off the trip, but only because I sold my house. Otherwise, I would be paying for it still, and that vacation was so long ago that I have forgotten the name of the camel I rode at the Pyramids. Anyway, now that I pay cash for all my vacations, I spend very little on trips out of town. So little that the monthly allotment looks pitiful on paper, and I know I need to up it, as Greece is calling.

Food was another interesting category. "I don't buy any food," I told Greg and Eric, confident on this one. "My refrigerator is full of leftovers from all the restaurants I visit on the job." I was certain that orange juice, milk and fresh fruit were all that I ever bought at the grocery. I was wrong.

When I admitted that the numbers I turned in may have been a tad misleading, Eric and Greg were gracious. They said there often is a difference between what people actually spend and what they think they spend. They suggested I write down all my expenses for several weeks.

That's how I found out how much money I spend on food, and that much of the spending isn't taking place at Dierbergs, the source of the aforementioned orange juice, milk and fresh fruit. In the past four weeks, I've bought dried fruit at the

Roasting House, olive bread at Great Harvest Bread, smoothies at St. Louis Smoothie and cinnamon-raisin bread at the St. Louis Bread Company. All that, and a few random lunches, belongs under food expenses.

I called Greg last week to discuss my 401K, and he asked how I was doing with my expense notebook. "You haven't stopped spending money, have you? Sometimes, when we ask people to record what they spend, they freeze up and stop spending," he said.

Oh no, I assured him. In fact, as soon as I got home from our second meeting, I had called to sign up for cable television. I wanted to be sure that expense was charged to the entertainment category before I found myself without any entertainment money. The day I got cable, the first channel I landed on was a shopping network. They were having a sale on a duvet cover, exactly the sort I was looking for to send to my son, so I bought it. The next day, I scored a few bargains at a half-of-half-off sale at my favorite fat-girl boutique.

No, I haven't stopped spending money. At this rate, at my next meeting with my financial advisers, I'll be short $1,100 a month.

October 2, 1999

OH-SO-FOND MEMORIES

Nobody gets through life without losing someone—or even many someones—they love. I've had many losses in my life, and here is what I have learned: If you treasure the memory of your loved ones, they never really leave you.

Sometimes, I open my mouth to speak and I hear a sentence that my mother used to say. In dreams, I sometimes hear my father laugh. And even when I'm awake, sometimes I hear my sardonic friend Ross whisper something delightfully catty in my ear.

This chapter celebrates the memories of people I love still, even though they are gone.

Mom

Mothers are suddenly dying. Bill's mother. Evan's mother. Rick's mother. There are flowers and donations to send, sympathy cards to write and memorial services to attend.

There are friends to hug and help get through it, friends to advise on how to get through it.

How long does it take to get over it, they ask.

I'll let you know, I say.

My mother died in 1973, when she was fifty-eight years old. I'm not over it.

I'm OK, of course, but remembering my mother, and missing her, is something I do often.

After nineteen years, there still are moments when warm memories of her come suddenly to mind, other moments when flashes of insight about her life occur, still other moments when I quote her on a variety of topics.

There are some moments when I ache, when I want my mother, when I am furious that she died.

There are times, too, when I think I am more self-reliant, more independent, more my own person than I ever would have been had I lived as an adult in the shadow of my mother.

Mothers, psychologists say, are the first and often the most significant role models for female children. Adult women whose mothers are still living often conduct their lives according to their mothers' values, morals and standards, rather than determining their own.

After all, if Mom is around to give advice on job seeking, husband hunting, home decorating, child rearing or whatever, most daughters are willing to hear it, and often to heed it.

"This is how my mother always did it," they say, as they wax baseboards or go to Wisconsin every summer or iron sheets or drive Fords or cover the pantry shelves with shelf paper or visit relatives every third Sunday or make turkey stuffing with cornbread.

That's tradition, for better or for worse.

The rest of us, those whose mothers died before we were fully formed as women, stumble along finding our own way, breaking new ground and starting new traditions.

We live our lives without our mothers around to say "I'm proud of you" or "I love you" or even "I told you so."

My mother died in her sleep, her life ended in the night by a massive heart attack. She had spent Sunday afternoon helping put down carpeting and hang drapes in my new house, just half a mile from my parents' home.

On Monday evening, we had talked briefly on the telephone after we both got home from work. I thanked her for her help and said I thought the house was coming along. She said she thought so too, and then she said she was very tired. We said goodnight.

At 5:30 a.m. Tuesday, the telephone rang. It was my father, who said to come over right away and then hung up. We drove up in front of their house fifteen minutes later, just in time to see two paramedics carrying my mother down the steps on a stretcher.

She was dead.

My son was born a year later. One day, when he was about four years old, we stopped at my dad's house to pick up something. My son had been in the house before, of course, and he had seen many pictures of my mother, but perhaps he hadn't been able to imagine her living there.

He was standing in the living room, looking around with an awakened sense of curiosity, when he said, "So Grandma lived here with Grandpa before she died?"

I said yes, and we started out the door. He put his hand in mine and said, "Grandma would have liked me."

Oh yes.

"Grandma" was planning to retire that year she died, to rest and travel and wait for the grandchildren that she wanted very much.

But she died, and I don't have a mother. Now, neither do Bill, Evan and Rick. My heart goes out to each of them.

March 14, 1992

Mike

On Mother's Day, I always think about kidney transplants, and what miracles they are.

My brother died of kidney failure on Mother's Day in 1963. He was two weeks shy of his tenth birthday. When he was five and I was ten, Michael Joseph Corrigan was diagnosed with nephritis, a degenerative disease of the kidneys. It took the disease five years to kill him.

In the early '60s, kidney transplants were still in the first stages of development and available to very few people. The life-saving immuno-suppressant drugs that now make all the difference in transplant operations had only just been introduced.

Dialysis, the procedure that removes toxins and immunities from the blood when the kidneys no longer perform that function, was still a complicated treatment used only on a limited basis.

There just wasn't much anyone could do.

Still, I have memories of a normal, happy childhood.

That's because my parents found the strength to put aside their own pain to make sure we did normal, happy things.

Mike and I had pets, we celebrated birthdays, we made many trips to the Zoo, we hung upside down on our backyard swing set, we learned to swim, we joined scout troops and we went on weekend fishing trips and modest family vacations every summer.

We spent hours singing songs from *The Mickey Mouse Club*, we worked hard on what to wear on Halloween night, we played hard with our cousins and our friends and we alternately provoked and protected our fox terrier, Buttons.

Of course, we also got into it periodically, as all sisters and brothers do. I still remember one horrid battle over a lunchbox.

I also remember trying once to beat up a neighborhood bully who was picking on Mike.

Most of the time, Mike seemed OK, though he was always pale.

Sometimes, he was in the hospital, undergoing various tests and rounds of experimental drugs. I wasn't allowed to visit him because at the time, hospitals didn't permit children on the patient floors.

Sometimes, a neighbor or a family friend would drive me and the family dog to the hospital, where I would stand under Mike's window, holding our pet, and wave up to him.

Toward the end, the nurses and staff looked the other way as my parents sneaked me up to Mike's room.

He died on Mother's Day, in 1963.

It was only years later that I grasped that viscerally.

I was walking through a shopping mall, pushing my three-month-old son along in his stroller. All of a sudden, out of nowhere, the thought crossed my mind that my mother had once had a baby boy and that he had died.

My entire body started to shake, and I felt as if I couldn't breathe. I had to stop and sit down and hold my own baby boy close until the moment passed.

Only then did I fully understand what my parents had been through, and what courage it took for them to go on living every day, providing as normal and happy a life as possible for my brother and me.

I do remember being told that Mike was very, very sick. I remember watching my parents take turns going to the hospital at all hours of the day and night. And I remember overhearing my mother tell a friend on the telephone that she thought we would "lose" Mike within a period of weeks.

And twenty-nine years later, I still remember exactly where I was and what I was doing when the call came from my parents at the hospital that Mike had died.

It was a sunny Sunday in May—Mother's Day.

Every year on Mother's Day, I always think about kidney transplants, and what miracles they are.

And, of course, I think about my little brother.

May 9, 1992

Aunt Jule and Aunt Julie

One of my great-aunts died three weeks before her 100th birthday.

At least we think that's how old she was.

The Mass card says she died three weeks before her ninety-ninth birthday. Lying there in her casket in a beautiful peach silk dress, she looked about seventy-five. Had she spoken, she might have insisted she was in her early sixties.

That's how she was—always young at heart and always determined that no one would find out just how young.

(The legendary Josephine Baker was the same sort of woman. Once, when asked her age, she replied, "I'm forty-two, not counting summers.")

Anyway, from earliest childhood on, I remember hearing discussions among my relatives regarding the age of Jule Corrigan Vollmer.

Some gauged her age by that of her daughter, who was born about the same time as my father. Others factored in my age and my cousin's age, because we were born the same year. Even her siblings argued, comparing dates and counting on their fingers.

And still Aunt Jule, as we called her, went on growing younger.

We children didn't really care. Aunt Jule always fussed over us and made all of us feel special.

She had tiny feet and tiny hands. At family parties, she allowed us to strut around in her high heels and try on the impressive rings she always wore. We put on her fur coat and breathed in her heady perfume, captured in the silk lining of the coat. We admired her manicure and her makeup.

Simply put, Aunt Jule personified gracious living. A trip to her big house, filled with beautiful treasures, was always a special treat.

She wasn't perfect—she did cheat at cards.

At family gatherings, after the dishes had been cleared, the women would sit down to a game of poker. From time to time, some of my uncles and male cousins would join them.

Invariably, the men would quit.

"Aunt Jule is cheating!" one of them would shout, pushing back from the table.

"I am not!"

"You are—you put in a nickel for a quarter bet. I saw you!"

Aunt Jule would smile engagingly.

"Oh, did I? I'm sorry. I didn't have my glasses on."

Then she would go right back to the game, neither adding to the pot nor putting on her glasses.

All through her life, one of Aunt Jule's closest friends was Julie Bock Corrigan, her sister-in-law. Aunt Julie, who proudly proclaims that she is ninety-one, is my other great-aunt, and she misses Aunt Jule a great deal.

"We talked every day, even after she moved into the nursing home. I went out to see her whenever I could," Aunt Julie said at the funeral home. "I sure miss her, Kid."

Aunt Julie has always called everyone "Kid."

She has never had furs or lavish jewelry or a big house, and she has never cared if people knew her age. But like Aunt Jule, Aunt Julie has the gift of making others feel special.

I remember a Sunday drive when I was about nine or ten, probably a trip to see Annie Mooney Corrigan, my paternal grandmother. Aunt Julie was in the car, and we stopped at a roadside produce stand. My mother and father bought some fresh corn for supper and some fruit for us kids.

Back in the car, Aunt Julie told us the name of the man who owned the produce stand, how long he'd had the stand, where his farm was, how much prices had gone up in the last year, how old his children were and that his wife was recovering from surgery.

She had forgotten to buy anything.

Sitting in the funeral home early in September, I was particularly grateful for the treasure that great-aunts are.

From one, I inherited terminal curiosity about the world and everyone in it. From the other, I got tiny feet, tiny hands and a sense of the importance of personal style.

Ageless gifts, all of those.

October 10, 1992

Daddy

"Dear Joseph Corrigan," the letter begins. "It may come down to the simple fact that you are running short of cash."

That's probably true. My father died ten years ago.

Joseph Timothy William Patrick Corrigan always carried a good amount of Cash—"walking around money," he called it—and he always shared it with anyone who needed it.

When he died, I ended up with that money and a wee bit more, and I've spent it all, so I can believe that Daddy is running short of cash.

Now this financial services institution has stepped forward to help him out with a little loan.

"Banc One Financial Services has a simple program to get you money fast," the letter reads. Right.

Fortunately, Daddy can apply by mail. Not that I think he'll be interested. Probably, he would get a good laugh out of it.

Daddy always laughed a lot, and he made others laugh, too. I learned from him to be suspicious of people who lack humor in their lives. (He also taught me the proper way to curse, but that's another story.)

It was always fun to listen to Daddy's stories; stories about the time he traded a horse for a bicycle, the many means he employed to provoke the nuns at St. Cronan's, his days as a Seabee, his spur-of-the-moment trips to Chicago to try out a new car.

Two days after the junk mail from Banc One showed up—the first mail of any kind to come to the house for him for a long, long time—Joseph Corrigan got another letter.

"There's a NEW MAGAZINE in America and it's named after YOU," says the teaser on the envelope.

I didn't even open this one, because the sender lied.

The name of the magazine, according to the back of the envelope, is not "Joseph T. W. P. Corrigan."

It's "Editorial Projects in Education," and the come-on is "Teachers with brains and self-respect have needed a publication like this for a long time."

Teachers?

With all due self-respect to teachers, my father drove a beer truck for Anheuser-Busch—a member in fine standing of Teamsters Local 133. We got lots of magazines (none for teachers that I recall), and we owned lots of books.

Daddy always read a lot. One summer, we both read every one of Ian Fleming's James Bond books. After that, we never could remember which plot twist was relevant in which book.

Many nights, Mom, Daddy and I all would show up at the dinner table with whatever books or magazines we were reading at the time. Sometimes, we'd share a pertinent paragraph or two. Sometimes, we'd eat in silence, each of us happily reading.

I threw the second piece of mail into a folder marked "Stuff" and forgot about it.

Three days passed. I came home from work to find a third piece of correspondence addressed to my father.

"Doctor's Astounding Secret Health Cures!" screams the type on the envelope.

The book advertised offers up "2,350 ASTONISHING HOME REMEDIES" plus these specific health tips, outlined on the envelope:

-Ease back pain with two pillows!

-Cure athlete's foot with ordinary baking soda!

-Rub aspirin on bee stings to stop pain!

Back pain? Bee stings? Astonishing home remedies?

It's a little late for that. He's gone, felled by far worse than athlete's foot, and no benevolent health tips will help him now.

But Joseph Timothy William Patrick Corrigan certainly has not been forgotten—and I'm not talking about his sudden presence on mailing lists.

Warm memories of his generosity, his spicy language, his love of books and his sense of humor live on.

February 27, 1993

Ross

Here's what happens when you die: Someone comes into your home and looks at every piece of paper in every drawer, searches for information on your bank accounts, your insurance policies, your wishes regarding the disposal of your possessions.

This is grueling work, grim at times and unexpectedly comical at others.

I know this because I did it last week. When one of my best friends died in a car accident, I cut short a vacation to join his sons and another friend in the necessary process.

I'm not talking here about fussing over who gets the food processor, who will take the plants or who could use a couch. That's stuff, and dealing with stuff comes later. Before that, the people left behind must make appointments with funeral directors, lawyers and accountants, and then they must find the information needed to begin to settle the estate.

For two long days, we combed through the buffet drawers, the kitchen drawers, the desk drawers. We riffled through stacks of paper on the dining room table, in the bedroom and tucked in between books on shelves.

We found exactly what we needed. We also found a form filled out to start a magazine subscription, a grocery list or two and a letter about a late fine for a parking ticket, paid up some six years ago. A stack of Christmas cards sat on top of the refrigerator. Letters from friends mingled with junk mail on the kitchen counter. Current bills stood waiting on the table.

As I sat sifting, I remembered that my friend once had initiated what he called a Paper Reduction Act. Several years ago, I was in the habit of sending him assorted clippings and cartoons that I knew he would enjoy. He called one day to announce he was no longer accepting such mail; that too many pieces of paper had found their way into his house and he was busily tidying up. At the time, I agreed to go along with his ruling, but I hadn't always kept my word.

Suddenly, I laughed aloud. At home on my cedar chest that very moment was a brochure I'd brought back for him from the Frank Lloyd Wright exhibit at the Museum of Modern Art and a short stack of articles I'd collected for him about that same exhibit. Now, those are mine to throw away or to move from place to place until someone has to come into my house and decide what to do with them.

I kept thinking I should go home and organize my important papers, maybe hang a note on the front door, or inside it at least, with directions on where to find the will, the credit cards, the bank account numbers, the insurance policies. Then, I should initiate a Paper Reduction Act, and keep no piece of paper past its time.

I'll do it immediately, I thought. But then the fatigue that accompanies great sorrow set in, and so far, I have shuffled no papers of my own.

Instead, I've spent idle moments reviewing the years I shared with this particular friend. I met him in 1981. He was intelligent, funny and totally bizarre—all qualities I appreciate in a man. I knew right away that he knew things I wanted to know, and I also knew he didn't want to share those things, as he was a very private person, often warm and loving only in spite of himself.

But I was up to the challenge. Over time, I earned my way into his life as a trusted friend. We cooked and ate many exquisite meals, we pored over maps searching for an island to retire to together and we laughed a lot.

A mutual friend once said we were perfect friends because we were both lonely in the same way, neither of us inclined to sacrifice our independence or alter our sometimes abrasive selves to suit someone else. And so we spent the better part of thirteen years on each other's minds, in each other's pockets, and in each other's hearts.

And now it's time to say goodbye to this dear friend.

Every time we left each other, he'd hug me and he'd kiss me, and then with a big wave, he'd call out this in parting: "Ciao, baby!"

Ciao.

March 26, 1994

CAUSES LOST AND FOUND

As a child of the '60s, I'm always looking for a good cause. And once I find one, of course, I'm eager to win others over to my point of view. Sometimes my causes are over big issues, and sometimes the issues haven't reached the mainstream. Sometimes I'm rational about my heartfelt beliefs and sometimes I'm not.

In any case, I am always earnest and I do mean well, so gather 'round as I climb onto my soapbox.

Pantyhose Can Kill

Pantyhose can kill.

OK—maybe not kill, but certainly maim for life.

Psychologically speaking, of course.

Why would any woman want to stuff her lower append-ages into unattractive, binding nylon tubes? Hasn't research proven that women who wear pantyhose too much develop an abiding fear of showing an unsheathed leg?

Surely that fear is triggered by tiny nylon filaments that insidiously enter the bloodstream.

Once, just once, I actually convinced a woman that was true.

Where is it written that females mustn't make do with socks in winter or go bare-legged in summer? What mania possesses us that we guilelessly run off to the store again and again to buy pantyhose in shades that no skin has ever approxi-mated, pantyhose that rip and run every time we put them on?

Listen to what Catherine Houck has to say about pantyhose in *The Fashion Encyclopedia*, her book full of fashion tips and history: "Sheer nylon pantyhose are probably one of the most foolish fashions in all history." She notes that they are cold in winter and hot in summer. And she brands them as ecologically irresponsible because they are made from petro-leum, a non-renewable resource.

"A far more sensible alternative is, whenever possible, bare legs and sandals in summer, midcalf skirts with knee-highs or boots, and wool/cotton thermal knee-length underwear in winter," Houck says. She also recommends wool or cotton tights in winter.

You just know Houck is a woman who follows her own

advice.

Would that women everywhere would follow her example and liberate themselves.

One particularly hot, sticky day a few weeks ago, I chided a colleague for wearing pantyhose.

"I have no choice," she said. "My legs are too white."

Too white for what?

This is the '90s. Tan is bad—it means you've been lying around in your backyard pretending you're at the beach, soaking up harmful rays.

Worse than legs clad in pantyhose that look like a bad varnish job are legs encased in wild patterns and designs. Remember when Julie Nixon Eisenhower proclaimed in the late '60s that she would never wear textured pantyhose because her husband, David, hated them?

It's too bad she couldn't make up her own mind, but at least she didn't appear at state functions in lacy, diamond-patterned pantyhose.

(This same woman later announced that she and David both would be proud to serve in Vietnam if anyone asked them. No one did ask, of course, but that's another story.)

Some women say they don't feel dressed up if they don't wear pantyhose. Some say they don't feel dressed at all. And some probably sleep in the silly things.

Pantyhose were introduced into the fashion market in the '60s as an alternative to stockings. They were slow to catch on, because clever women noticed right away that all "one-size-fits-all" pantyhose fit no one.

Now pantyhose come in a full range of sizes. But they still are relentlessly, totally tubular. Legs—most legs, anyway—taper as they wend their way south from the thigh to the ankle.

How they fit anyone's budget is also a mystery. Some women actually buy them by the dozen, and keep spare pairs in their desks and in their cars. (Speaking of cars, don't forget that pantyhose make great emergency substitutions for broken fan belts.)

Pantyhose simply don't last.

Well—I do have a pair that I bought seventeen years ago. Of course, I've never taken them out of the package.

I'm saving them for a time capsule of this strange, misguided era in fashion.

June 13, 1992

Ghost of Gaslight

The ghost of Gaslight Square made a brief appearance last weekend.

How else to explain a little dancing in the street, a spontaneous eruption of delight just outside the Sheldon late last Friday night?

The dancer in question was a grown-up, a woman who for just a few minutes transcended the uncertainty of modern life and broke out in a fit of gleeful dancing on her way from the ballroom to her car.

Who the woman was (and it was not me, although I have done more than my share of dancing in streets) is not important.

The occasion was the end of a remarkable evening spent reveling in the music—indeed, the life—of one Jeanne Trevor, who is starring in Theater Factory's production of *Jeanne Trevor: St. Louis Woman*.

In the show, Trevor musically recounts the chronology of her life, which includes time spent in Harlem, on the West Coast and in St. Louis. She sings blues, ballads, jazz, opera, scat and show tunes, warming every heart in the house with each

66

number.

Throughout the evening, Trevor talks of the glory days of Gaslight Square, and it was Gaslight Square that was on the minds of many as they left the show.

Climbing down the many steps at the Sheldon, humming snatches of favorite tunes from the evening, people suddenly started telling friends and strangers alike about their experiences at Gaslight Square, vividly recounting thirty-year-old memories.

A woman behind me told of going to the clubs and coffee houses, a man ahead of me spoke of the restaurants and bars, another man on the stairs spoke wistfully of the talent that had come through town to play Gaslight Square.

One younger woman sighed and said she deeply regretted missing "the good old days" in St. Louis, but she remembered hearing her parents speak of many good times in Gaslight.

I missed most of the action myself. As a teen-ager in the mid-'60s, I made but two trips to the legendary area; once to see a Chekhov play in a little second-floor theater, and once to dine in the fading elegance at the Three Fountains restaurant.

A few years later, I discovered O'Connell's, the last hold-out in the old neighborhood, and it was there that I was introduced to Irish whiskey.

But according to those who know, there once was a vibrant entertainment district here, where musicians, composers, playwrights, performers and poets alike made the fruits of their labor available to anyone who meandered in for an evening.

It all took place not too far from the Sheldon, which sits on Washington just west of Grand.

It took place in a time when we were first in booze, first in shoes and not worth mentioning in regard to the American League.

And it took place in a time when people were interested in—not afraid of—what practitioners of the performing arts had to say.

The music, the memories, Jeanne Trevor's richly layered performance delivered to a crowd of mixed races and ages sitting together on a soft summer's night—maybe all the elements conspired and brought to life for just a moment a hint of what once was.

For just a moment there, the air shimmered, and all of us could imagine that we had numerous choices about where to go next at 10:45 p.m. on a Friday in St. Louis.

We had just heard Trevor, and we could imagine that artists of her caliber were playing in dozens of sophisticated late-night clubs where we could drop in for a couple of hours.

We could imagine coffee houses, bars, restaurants—all nearby and all inviting.

We could imagine all this most vividly, because there in the moonlight, outside the Sheldon, we saw the ghost of Gaslight Square.

Dancing.

August 29, 1992

Helium Balloons

Read my lips: NO MORE HELIUM BALLOONS.

They're everywhere in this Year of the Presidential Election—hundreds of thousands of red, white and blue helium-filled balloons streaming up into the sky at every political rally, speech and media event.

People who would never drop a piece of paper on the street or throw a can out of a car window think nothing of setting free a balloon that will end up as just another piece of litter.

This litter is like no other. The balloons travel hundreds of miles from their launch sites.

In 1988, a balloon that had been released from St. Louis was found by a woman on Sable Island—ninety miles off the coast of Canada in the Atlantic Ocean. The balloon had traveled 1,300 air miles. Another balloon tagged with the name of a resident of Neah Bay, Washington, ended up in Jasper National Park in Alberta, Canada.

The Center for Marine Conservation in Washington, D.C., collects and tallies trash found on beaches. In 1989, volunteers picked up 18,251 balloons—in a three-hour period.

Not all of them end up on beaches. Some of the spent balloons have been responsible for the deaths of marine mammals, sea turtles and birds.

The Marine Mammal Stranding Center in Brigantine, New Jersey, found a balloon blocking the entrance to the intestines of a dead sperm whale. The animal had died of starvation. Dead seabirds have been found with balloons tangled around their beaks.

Sea turtles eat balloons. In 1987, a dead leatherback sea turtle was found with a single balloon in its stomach. The knot in the balloon was blocking where the stomach and intestines meet. A three-foot blue ribbon extended into the intestines.

Is the few seconds spent watching a balloon float away worth the life of a whale, a turtle or a bird?

People in Connecticut, Tennessee and Florida don't think so. Those states have outlawed the release of helium-filled balloons. Baltimore and Louisville have passed laws prohibiting balloon releases. Schools in Philadelphia have a "no balloon release" policy. Officials at the University of Alabama have stopped the release of balloons at football games.

The National Park Service prohibits the release of helium-filled balloons at all 354 sites.

A directive issued in 1989 states, "The National Park Service will not permit the sale or use of helium-filled latex or Mylar balloons unless they can be controlled or recovered."

Even the National Science Foundation canceled an annual balloon launch that took place from 1985 through 1989 as part of National Science and Technology Week.

Each year, thousands of elementary school students launched balloons as part of an experiment tracking weather patterns. Environmentalists protested mightily, and the project was dropped.

I'm guilty.

Fourteen years ago, I helped release a helium-filled balloon on a cold New Year's Eve night. Everyone at the party wrote down something they wanted to let go of, and we attached the note to the balloon before we launched it.

An old-fashioned resolution, put in writing or expressed aloud, would have accomplished the same thing.

Who gets hurt if people attending political rallies, ball games, charity fund-raisers or parties don't send off pretty balloons?

The balloon industry.

"We're not anti-balloon," said Lisa Younger, who works for the Center for Marine Conservation.

"We recommend celebrating with indoor balloon releases or balloon sculptures or decorations made from balloons," she said. "If you buy a balloon for a child, tie it on his or her wrist to make sure it stays put."

Then everybody stays happy and more wild creatures stay alive.

No more helium balloons—please.

October 17, 1992

We All Can Dance

Last weekend, we all performed in a dance concert, every one of us. We glided, we twirled, we leapt across the stage, strong and lithe, interpreting complicated choreography with grace, skill and depth of feeling.

Of course, we weren't literally on that stage. Mid America Dance Company presented the concert, and the MADCO dancers did the actual gliding, twirling, leaping and interpreting.

But somewhere in the middle of the concert, I realized that we who are not professional dancers can live vicariously—gloriously so—through those who are.

Think about it a minute.

How many times have you watched an individual dancer and been filled with a deep appreciation for the art itself as well as the artist? Or maybe you were at the symphony, exhilarated by a flute solo.

Either way, when the individual performer communicates all the beauty and power of the moment and we in the audience get that message, somehow we're all part of that moment together.

Of course, we can't be Stacy West or the other MADCO dancers. But if we watch intently, follow every move, we can experience dance vicariously, imagining that we are Stacy West.

I don't know this, but I suspect a different part of the brain engages when we watch dance or we hear music. Maybe the endorphins, those pleasure-giving amino acids that are responsible for runner's high, have something to do with it.

Maybe this also explains why some people get their kicks

watching professional athletes play. I can't say for sure, because snorkeling is my sport, and watching someone snorkel is silly. But the transfer, the blurring or blending of roles between the performer and the audience, seems possible only when no words are spoken.

Good theater, or a gripping moment in an exceptional movie, can transport an audience, but I'm betting some additional brain function kicks in when we hear the spoken word, some function that allows us to comprehend the meaning of the words we hear.

An exception might be opera that is not sung in one's native language. A friend who loves opera listened to me complain one day that appreciation of opera eludes me because I can't understand anything anyone is singing.

"That doesn't matter if it's good opera," he said. "After a few minutes, you forget that you don't know Italian or German, and somehow, you understand anyway."

Appreciating dance or music takes a few minutes, too.

First, you have to get past anxiety, the fear that you will be the only person in the room who doesn't know what you're looking at or hearing. You have to quickly dispense with intellectual exercises. It just doesn't matter, for the moment, if you understand how the musician plays the instrument or the dancer executes the movement.

And you must move past envy.

It's OK to spend a few seconds admiring a dancer's body or a musician's flair. But if you pause long enough to worry why you don't look like that or can't play like that, you may find yourself disliking the performer.

"Just look at that gorgeous body. I hate her," you may think.

Hating her may keep you from appreciating what she's worked so hard learning to do well.

What point is there in that? Part of the pleasure of life is appreciating other people for who they are and what gifts they possess. Allowing that does not detract at all from who we are and what we do well.

Besides, if envy sits next to you at any concert, you'll miss that wonderful moment that comes when you shut down your busy brain and allow your senses to take over.

Then, you'll discover that dancers tell our body's secrets and musicians speak for our souls. You'll discover that whether you can dance a step or play a note, you can be part of the experience, vicariously.

Suddenly, you'll be gliding, twirling, leaping . . .
March 13, 1993

Remember the ICU

The people sitting right this minute in the intensive care unit waiting rooms in hospitals do just that—they wait.

They wait for two-hour blocks of time to pass, so they may spend fifteen minutes at the bedside of a relative in the ICU. They wait for a doctor to come with news. They wait for other family members and friends to show up and sit for a while with them.

While they wait, they talk softly among themselves. Sometimes, they sit silently. They stare vacantly at the wall. They flip through magazines. They turn up the television set and then neglect to watch the program.

They take turns answering the telephone, carefully writing down any message if the party receiving the call is out of the room.

Sometimes, they give in just briefly to the emotional strain caused by all the waiting—and the reason for having to wait in the first place—and they cry softly. Rarely does anyone break down.

I know all this because I spent several days in an ICU waiting room earlier this month with the family of a close friend.

Sitting there, hour after hour, I was embarrassed to realize that I'd never thought about ICU waiting rooms or the people waiting there until I was in one. Human dramas, angst-ridden matters of life and death, play out in these rooms every day, in hospitals all over this city and every other city.

No matter what sort of lives the people in the rooms were living yesterday, they have set those lives aside now to come sit and wait. No matter what the outcome for the specific patient, the lives of those in the waiting room also change forever. And no matter what emotional price those who wait must pay, they pay it in the company of strangers.

The individual families rarely mingle, rarely interrupt or interfere with other families in the waiting room. Yet everyone there is part of an odd little community, one in which the members change from day to day.

No one formally moves from group to group, making introductions or asking about particulars. Yet, over time, everyone learns at least first names, and comes to know why everyone else is there.

"How is your mom doing?" one will ask another.

"Fine, coming along. And what about your husband?" is the reply.

Strangers, all depending on the small kindnesses of other strangers.

For most of those sitting in the waiting room, the ICU nurses and staff members also are strangers; strangers entrusted with the lives of loved ones.

In most instances, those strangers are forgotten once the

patient improves and moves to another floor of the hospital. Then, after a stay on a regular nursing unit, the patient checks out, often leaving behind some of the gifts of food and plants he or she received while ill.

"The floor nurses always get goodies," said a floor nurse I know who has spent more than her fair share of time lately in ICU waiting rooms. "When you have someone in the ICU, you're under so much stress that you overlook the ICU nurses, who are the commandos of hospital medicine."

In other words, even people who have thought about ICU nurses and ICU waiting rooms because once they waited there don't necessarily think about them afterward.

Here's what I think about that: Thursday is Thanksgiving. Maybe everyone who has ever sat for tension-filled hours in an ICU waiting room—or been a patient in an intensive care unit—might head for the nearest hospital (regardless of where you did your time) and drop off a platter for the ICU staff of anything you'd like to see on a platter waiting with your name on it.

In this way, we can thank some important strangers who made a difference in our lives.

One more thought: Don't forget the night shift.
November 19, 1994

Whales vs. People

Esrichtius Robustus may not be so "robustus" much longer.

Gray whales soon may be under attack at two points during their annual migration from the Bering and Chukchi seas south to Baja California, Mexico.

In Neah Bay, Washington, members of the Makah Indian

nation hope to take up whaling after a seventy-year respite. Farther south, the Mexican government is considering a proposal to set up a salt production plant in San Ignacio Lagoon, where gray whales breed and give birth. If the plant is built, it could produce six million tons of salt each year, resulting in sales of about $100 million a year.

The Makah blame unemployment and depression in their community of 1,800 for their problems with alcohol, drugs, crime and domestic violence. They say killing whales will alleviate some of those problems.

"Whaling will build sagging self-esteem," the tribal general manager told a Seattle newspaper. "It will build pride and remind us of who we are."

Ironically, the gray whales are one of the conservationists' success stories.

Whalers wiped out the North Atlantic population, but the North Pacific populations have recovered twice from near-extinction. In the mid-nineteenth century, so many gray whales were slaughtered that eventually they were classified as "economically extinct," which meant there were so few, it wasn't worth the time or trouble to hunt them.

Left alone, the species began to recover, only to be nearly wiped out again in modern times with the advent of mechanized whaling techniques. The U.S. and Mexican governments stepped in to protect the animals, and today, about 23,000 gray whales make the annual migration.

You may remember the international effort in the fall of 1988 to save three whales trapped in the ice off Point Barrow, Alaska. Those were gray whales. And if you've ever seen a photo of someone petting a whale, the picture probably was taken off the coast of Baja California, in the quiet lagoons where gray whales approach small boats full of whale watchers.

I've been in those boats in San Ignacio Lagoon. I've petted gray whales, and I've leaned way out of the boat to hug them. I've even planted a big, Blistex-smeared kiss on one adolescent female whale that spent three hours next to the boat one sunny morning.

These are experiences I will never forget: sacred moments that taught me what a privilege it is to interact with a wild animal.

Gray whales grow to lengths of forty-five to fifty feet and weigh about a ton per foot. Their stocky bodies, flippers and flukes are mottled with gray and white splotches. Their spouts are easily recognizable, as the blows resemble heart-shaped puffs of steam.

The Makah say they have the right to hunt gray whales under provisions of a treaty signed in 1855 with the U.S. They say they will work with the International Whaling Commission before they begin.

Ten years ago, the Commission banned commercial whaling. Japan, Norway and Iceland have defied the Commission and continue to slaughter whales. The Makah have announced they will consult with commercial whalers in those three countries, though they insist they have no plans to sell any whale meat.

Currently, whale meat sells for as much as $100 a kilo in Japan.

An expert in anthropological linguistics who is married to a Makah told the *Seattle Post-Intelligencer*: "If this community had access to all of its traditional activities, there is a good chance that it would be a healthier community than it is now."

Let's hope that the Makah heal their community and that Mexico boosts its troubled economy in ways that don't harm the magnificent gray whales.

June 24, 1995

Punctuation Goes to Hell

For my money, public signage has reached a new high in low.

Take those billboards all over town advertising a local bank. They feature a close-up photo of a greasy-haired woman with the words "For my money it's BANK NAME HERE."

You've seen the billboards; I don't need to name the bank.

Though I wish the model had washed her hair before doing the photo shoot, that's not my primary objection to the sign. No, what's particularly irritating about these billboards is what's missing.

Namely, a comma.

Where I come from, a comma is in order after the words "For my money." I confess I don't remember the specific rule about this, but I do remember a comma is called for, and its omission is enough to make me want to scramble up the billboard and draw one in.

I also remember a note I received once, from a new friend.

"Gosh," he wrote, "it seems almost intimidating to write a note to a writer. I hope all my punctuation is in the right place."

It was, and I told him so.

He confessed to a life-long insecurity about where to place commas. I suggested he read aloud whatever he writes, and drop in commas wherever he paused. (He's turned into a delightful comma-maniac, littering everything he writes with dramatic pauses, but that's another story.)

If you apply that technique to the phrase on the ubiquitous billboards, you'll just ache to slide a comma in between the word "money" and the bank's name.

My friend Richard also notices absent commas on signs, but he is more often on the lookout for apostrophe abuse. It's widespread.

"It seems that no one is certain anymore where to put an apostrophe," he says. "I call this syndrome 'apostrophobia.'"

Apostrophes (which are airborne commas) are used to indicate the omission of a letter or letters from a word or phrase (o' for of or it's for it is); to form the possessive case (Elspeth's elephant); and to form some plurals (five 6's or three i's).

So says the dictionary, which is no slouch when it comes to grammar.

Anyway, Richard finds new examples of apostrophe abuse daily, and he enjoys them immensely. On signs, in brochures, in newspapers (ouch!), everywhere, plural words boldly become possessive. For instance, I saw this sign at the produce market: "Kiwi's, 4 for $1."

Our favorite example to date is this, discovered at the bottom of a direct-mail letter: "Thank's."

Another friend, sometimes prone to editing even private conversation, takes particular exception to geographic disarray. One November day, we were walking through the Climatron at the Missouri Botanical Garden, enjoying the illusion that we were in a tropical clime. We stopped to admire a plant native to the Seychelles, a country made up of islands in the Indian Ocean.

His face flushed when he read the sign next to the plant.

"This says the Seychelles are northwest of Madagascar. That's ridiculous," he said. "They are northeast."

Before I could call up a map of Madagascar in my mind to see if I agreed with him, he pulled up the sign and stalked off, muttering about finding someone in the education department to correct the error. I went after him and convinced him to put the sign back. I said we could stop in the education department later, on our way out.

He finally agreed, but he asked to borrow the red pen I always carry just for this purpose. (I once corrected three different misspellings of "croissant," all on the same menu.) I gave him the pen. He scratched out the offending word and wrote in the right location for the Seychelles. We went on with our day.

Some people collect matchbooks, some play golf and some of us enjoy watching out for wayward punctuation and funky fact errors. If you share this hobby, feel free to send along some of your favorite examples.

Thank's.

September 30, 1995

World AIDS Day

Monday is World AIDS Day, a day set aside to raise awareness of the disease. Of course, those of us who love someone with AIDS think about it every day, but we're pleased that the rest of you join us on December 1.

My friend Philip has AIDS, and he's never far from my thoughts. That's not to say that my thoughts about Philip are routinely grim and depressing. On the contrary—Philip does not personify the disease, because although he has accommodated AIDS as part of his life, he has not become the disease or allowed it to control his life. Mostly, I think about Philip a lot because he has taught me so much about how to live.

Philip is thirty-four. I met him early in 1995, when I first became friends with his brother Edward. Philip works full time, but to protect his privacy, I'm not saying where. He was diagnosed with full-blown AIDS in April of 1992, which makes him a long-term survivor. When he was tested for AIDS and learned that he was positive, he realized that was what he had expected to hear, as it explained a case of shingles he had endured the previous summer.

Now, he takes twenty-four pills a day, spending more than $15,000 a year on drugs to fight the virus and fend off infection, something his damaged immune system is incapable of doing. Philip copes with numerous unpleasant side effects, including nerve damage in his legs, from the many drugs he takes. He hasn't been hungry for four years—another side effect—and though he eats nutritious meals, he has lost more than fifty pounds. Frequent trips to the gym keep him strong, and fortunately, Philip has yet to experience a medical crisis that has required that he go in the hospital.

For all these reasons, I routinely remember Philip in my prayers. But most often I think about him because he has said something profound or funny or intriguing. For instance, when someone asked whether he was going to die of AIDS, Philip responded, "It would be foolish to think that I would survive it. I've come to grips with dying. I was going to do it anyway, eventually, so it's never been much of an issue."

See? That's profound, funny and intriguing all at the same time.

Still, Philip admits that having AIDS has changed his life.

For instance, unlike most thirty-four-year-olds, he has made a will, filed a signed health directive with his doctor and made plans for his memorial service. Once all that was in order, Philip turned his attention from dying to living.

"It's now a joy to wake up every morning, and I truly cherish every minute of every day," he said. "You shouldn't have to be terminally ill to learn that, but that's often the case."

Two years ago, when I was diagnosed with breast cancer, Philip wasted no words. "You'll come to think of this as an opportunity to learn more about living," he said, quieting my sobs. Later, when I blurted out that I didn't particularly like the statistics that now predict my future, Philip replied with great glee, "I'll trade my numbers for yours any day."

The day before my surgery, we went to the Zoo together. Philip knew much that I needed to know, and he was completely frank with me, completely willing to share his wisdom. And, as always, he made me laugh. To this day, he remains part of my extended family, and I am proud to be part of his.

Philip says that he can't ever forget that he has AIDS, though he relegates it to a "back burner" mentally, so that he spends little time thinking about it. That is why Philip accomplishes more in the course of a day than most of us. Of course, the disease is uppermost in his mind after a discouraging report from the doctor. When that happens, Philip gets upset and so does his partner, who has been with him since eight months before the diagnosis.

"We get mad over a bad report, and then we get over it," said Philip.

"I may not get all the time in the world that I want to spend with Philip," said his partner, "but we try to make good use of the time we have."

This week, Philip is spending time fretting because he hasn't bought Christmas cards yet, rejoicing because he just learned that his sister is pregnant and nagging because his brother won't come to the gym with him more often.

Also, Philip is thinking about World AIDS Day. What he's thinking is that it's OK to let me tell his story, something I've wanted to do for a long time.

"I hope you don't write about me because you think I'm some kind of hero. I'm not. There are days when I am totally

82

ill-behaved," Philip said, laughing. "But you could say that the generations following mine should not have to experience AIDS. We now know enough about preventing this disease that no one should go through this in the future."

Something to think about on World AIDS Day, 1997.
November 29, 1997

Weighty Guidelines

So—have you lost 10 percent of your body weight yet?

Hey, the government is counting on you. A division of the National Institutes of Health once again has revised the national weight guidelines, and now half of all Americans, instead of just a third of us, are too fat.

Those of us the government finds unacceptable have been asked to lower our body mass index, a calculation that reeks of voodoo mathematics if I ever saw one. To get your BMI, you multiply your weight by 703 and then divide by your height in inches squared, a formula that also works if you're figuring what you need for retirement. Factor in your street address and your mother's maiden name, and maybe you'll discover whether you are fat, which may or may not come as a surprise.

Never mind that there is not enough scientific evidence to support that obesity actually causes the diseases sometimes associated with it. Because of that, an editorial in the *New England Journal of Health* in January urged doctors to ease up on pushing people to lose weight.

Never mind that there is no scientific evidence that a fat person who loses weight will live longer than a person who has never been overweight.

Never mind that two years ago, researchers, public health officials and drug companies made available a combination of diet drugs that were found to cause primary pulmonary hypertension, neurotoxicity and valvular heart disease. Now a new diet drug, Meridia, has received approval from the U.S. Food and Drug Administration against the recommendation of the FDA's own advisory panel.

Never mind that the National Institutes of Health reported in 1992 that dietary and behavioral treatments for weight loss have a 95 percent failure rate.

In other words, never mind the facts.

A spokeswoman for the NIH was all over every front page recently, proclaiming the dangers of obesity and saying, "Weight loss is possible." Who backed her up? Dr. Richard Atkinson, who is affiliated with the American Obesity Association, an agency funded by the commercial diet industry, which rakes in $33 billion each year in spite of that 95 percent failure rate.

Cynical? Me? Just because I believe the new guidelines are based on corporate greed instead of any real concern for health? Fitness and good health are worthy goals for all of us, fat or thin or in between, but I reject the notion that being overweight is a disease, and I resent this effort to make it one. Pregnancy and menopause are two other natural occurrences in life that this odd country now considers medical issues, and American plastic surgeons have gone so far as to declare small breasts a "deformity."

The National Association to Advance Fat Acceptance, a nonprofit organization, has called the government's new clinical guidelines "ludicrous and dangerous" and chides the NIH for creating public health policy that focuses on weight loss rather than on improving health.

Cheri K. Erdman, author of *Nothing To Lose: A Guide to Sane Living in a Larger Body* and *Live Large: Ideas, Affirmation and Actions for Sane Living in a Larger Body*, both published by HarperCollins, notes that if the government and the medical establishment succeed in defining fatness as a disease, then they will have to find a cure—or maybe even tax large people for "extra" pounds.

"By declaring that 50 percent of all Americans are overweight, they can say they have a health emergency, an epidemic, and that will justify giving more money to pharmaceutical companies to find a cure," Erdman said last week from her office in Glen Ellyn, Illinois, where she is a counselor and professor at the College of DuPage. "First, they create the problem, arbitrarily designating fatness as a disease, and then they go to work to create a solution."

Erdman, a large woman, said she suspects that some people who look at her may imagine that she is unhealthy because she is big. On the contrary, she is quite fit, swimming laps and walking for the past twenty years. "After spending thirty years as a professional dieter, I finally learned to quit listening to the so-called experts and start listening to my body, paying attention to my health instead of my size," Erdman said.

"In that thirty years, I noticed that the government often changed its dietary guidelines. First, it was don't eat eggs, then it was do eat eggs. We were told to stay away from butter, and then we were told that eating margarine was worse than butter. Red wine was out, then it was in," she said.

"To this day, there are no clear guidelines on what obesity or overweight means, and now government agencies and medical groups all are contradicting one another. Let them fight with each other—I don't care what they say," Erdman concluded.

June 20, 1998

PARENTING WITHOUT A LICENSE

One day, some friends were sitting around discussing our various nicknames, names other people had given us through the years. I listed some of mine: Corri, Whale Goddess, Irish, Ginkgo Goddess, p.c., Voluptua. . . . Suddenly, a thought drifted through my mind and I shivered at the power of its truth.

"I know my favorite name that anyone has ever called me," I announced.

"What?" my friends asked.

"Mom."

Only one person calls me that, and he is the person I love most in the world—Joel, my son. Over the years, I have written a lot of columns about our evolving relationship, and over the years, Joel has consistently wished I wouldn't do that. He gets embarrassed, even mad, when strangers rush up to us and say, "And you must be Joel!" He claims that he never wanted to be recognized in public, even if I enjoy it.

Joel feels so strongly about this that he suggested I refer to him as Sam in the columns printed in this book.

"It's too late," I told him. "You are Joel and everybody knows it."

We all parent without a license or much in the way of training. Most of us try to do our best. I certainly did—even if sometimes I discussed my parenting efforts in a public forum.

Fired from the Best Job

I've been fired.

Not from my job at the newspaper—from my job as a mother.

I am one of the many newly unemployed parents of high school seniors. Not only are we out of work, we are regarded by our children as ignoramuses and nuisances.

And that's on good days.

We had been warned about the pain and pride that comes with an empty nest. But warnings about this earlier stage somehow escaped our notice. Suddenly we find ourselves living with Senior Men and Women moving through the last stages of the transition from childhood to adulthood.

As they struggle to cut family ties, we struggle to let them go gracefully into the world we've tried so hard to prepare them for.

All this struggling makes for turbulent times for everyone concerned.

On some days, the contents of our wallets hold some interest for our children; other days, they fancy the four-wheeled vehicles that we own.

Some days, we are completely invisible, of no use whatsoever, unworthy of even a sneer in passing from our formerly charming children.

How did this happen?

For one thing, most members of my generation taught our children to question authority.

We failed to realize we would be the first authorities they questioned.

Make no mistake—we love them. Maybe we have loved

them too well.

We are the generation that came from parents who were determined that we would not suffer the hardships they had suffered. Most of their dreams for us came true, and we forged ahead into parenthood ourselves full of the energy and generosity that characterizes our generation.

We came of age during the Summer of Love, but our children were most influenced by the Me Decade.

No matter what we gave them, it never seemed to be enough, so we gave them more, offering up important words to live by along with another Esprit sweater or a second pair of Oakley sunglasses.

We bought them stereos, computers, expensive jewelry, CD players, futons, in-line skates, wardrobes of fun watches and most everything else they wanted. Most of us held out when it came to buying them cars of their own, but some of us succumbed even to that.

And now all the stuff, all the designer clothes and all the huge shoes lie piled up in our children's rooms; those same rooms where dozens of letters from college admissions offices now lie half under the bed, unopened.

Where are our children?

Out practicing being adults, gearing up to leave us for good.

By now, most of us have eased up on the rules, backed down on the curfew and agreed to let our children make most decisions for themselves.

When they take us at our word on all that—and usually we do mean it—we sit at home wondering what we may have forgotten to tell them, what secrets of survival or lessons of life we may have neglected to teach.

We know it's too late, of course.

It's too late because our services—and our advice—are

no longer required.

We've been fired, laid off from our jobs after eighteen years of working twenty-four-hour shifts, seven days a week.

We are grateful when our sons and daughters actually initiate a meaningful conversation with us, we delight in an unexpected hug, we beam at the most back-handed of compliments.

We are getting through this as best we can, taking it one day at a time, trying not to dwell on the shocking notion that this is our last year together in the same house, our last chance to practice the fine art of parenting on these tall young men and women.

We know that this difficult period is a most necessary stage; we even remember going through it ourselves.

Seniors—please remember this is a transitional year for us, too.

And we miss you already.

September 26, 1992

Eternal Safety Net

Don't think of it, a friend said, as losing a son. Think of it as gaining a closet.

And so my son has gone off to college.

All summer, I've wondered how I would handle The Day. This is no small event in our lives. Big changes are required of each of us. We both must begin again, learn different roles in our relationship and in the world.

The Day was fine, thank you. More about that later.

The summer in general was ridiculous. Time after time, I found myself missing Joel, even though he was still at home. I take comfort in knowing that I'm not the only parent who choked back tears, sometimes in public, at inappropriate moments.

While picking up some last-minute things at the mall for her son, a friend found herself staring at college-bound students in the stores. She knew none of them, but tears rolled down her face. This same friend happened to be home alone when one of her son's pals called to say he was off to school. "I'm all packed and ready," the young man said. "Earlier this summer, I was kind of scared about starting college, but now I'm really excited."

She wished him well, wiping away unbidden tears. Me, I cried at the movies and at the theater. At a showing of *A River Runs Through It*, I got teary when the older son opens his acceptance letter from the faraway college of his choice. Then I cried during a performance of *Mame*, when a grown-up Patrick Dennis sings "My Best Girl" on the telephone to his Auntie Mame.

The day before my son left, I got up and wrote this letter to him:

Dear Joel,

You say you know all my maxims, parables, life lessons and anecdotes. You say we don't need to review them now that you are leaving for college.

OK.

You have a big brain (as Kurt Vonnegut would say), and I know you will use it well. But I can't resist just a quick reminder that it is your responsibility to live an exciting life. Ruts can be cozy, a false sense of security can comfort, the known can appear more appealing than the unknown.

Guard against all that. I am, of course, talking cumulatively here—we both know the mind and the body need some down time, time to replenish. But then get back to it; make the most of your opportunities.

My five watchwords are these: Yes, Now, Go, Be and Do. Whenever you are confronted with a choice that offers a challenge, a learning opportunity, or a wonderful adventure that does no harm to people, animals, or the earth, answer with one of those five words.

Let yourself grow, even—maybe especially—if it seems as if it might be a hassle. I'm your safety net, here whenever you need me. I'm on your side. I love you.

Now, Go.

Then I went to the office, where I yelled at everybody. Later, I got sent home for crying.

On The Day, we packed the car, picked up Joel's best friend and headed north. We didn't talk much. Instead, we played the score to *Les Miserables*, and we all sang loudly along.

On campus, student guides unloaded the car and took us to Joel's dorm room. We went out for lunch. We walked around the quadrangle. Then we returned to the dorm, and my son began to unpack.

(At no time did I tell Joel how to organize his things. I know a mother who, two weeks ago at another college, nervously counseled her son on how to hang up his clothes a certain way. Of course, she was just talking to keep from thinking about saying goodbye, but her loving family told her to shut up.)

After about an hour, Joel looked around the tiny room and at his things in it, and he said with some satisfaction, "I can do this."

I can, too.

I'll start by moving my slide projector and umpteen boxes of slides into my new closet.

August 28, 1993

The College Freshman

All you parents of first-year college students are keeping all those letters you're getting, right?

Ha! If only we were getting letters. . . .

Nobody writes letters anymore. Lovers, diplomats and literary figures don't write letters, so why should college students?

It's so much easier to phone home. Have you considered keeping those messages left on the answering machine, bundling up those precious tiny tapes that represent the sole communication between you and your offspring?

Neither have I.

I have paid one visit to my son. Before I headed north to his college campus, I told myself that I must not hold an inquisition once there. I must go as a nonjudgmental observer with pleasant mannerisms, expecting little information other than that which I gathered intuitively.

I decided to approach Joel as if he were a newly independent country, not yet weaned from colonial support, but making the effort nonetheless.

"So," I said shortly after arriving, "how is independence working out for you?"

"Fine," he said.

I tried a more personal approach, speaking as if I were someone else's mother.

"Remember sorting through the hundreds of college brochures, narrowing down the possibilities, applying to just a few and then choosing among the three that interested you? Did you make the right decision?"

"Yes," he said.

I asked about his social life. He pretended he hadn't heard me.

I'd make a terrible spy.

After a few hours, Joel did talk more freely about his classes and the guys in the dorm. I asked if he had joined any campus organizations.

"I went to Quad Day, where more than 400 organizations had booths," he said. "I joined the Flying Illini."

I asked what that group does.

"Skydiving," he said calmly. "I've always wanted to go skydiving, and now I'm doing it."

I immediately pushed from my mind the terrifying image of my son jumping out of an airplane.

But what could I say? I'm the person who wrote him a letter when he left for school, a letter that said flat out: "It is your responsibility to live an exciting life . . ."

Joel noted my silence.

"You can't tell me not to do it," he said.

"I don't intend to tell you not to do it."

"I'm not going to die jumping out of a plane."

"I don't think you're going to die."

"You're too quiet. What are you thinking?" he asked.

"I'm thinking about the money. Skydiving is an expensive sport, and you've already spent all the money you made this summer."

"So have you," he said.

We declared a truce and went out to dinner.

Last week, on his birthday, I called Joel throughout the day, leaving messages on his answering machine. I had sent him a chocolate dinosaur and five different cards, with twenty dollars tucked in each.

Still, I wanted to talk to my only child on his nineteenth birthday. By late afternoon, he had not called me. I whined about it aloud at the office.

"You need to let go," said a colleague. "He's a man now."

This, from a father who drives 500 miles every three months to change the oil in his daughter's car.

Undaunted, I called Joel one more time. I finally came up with a message that merited a return call from my busy student:

"It may be your birthday, but I am the person who had the baby. Call me."

A letter couldn't have said it any better.

October 23, 1993

You're Going to Buy a What?

After years of unsuccessful attempts, my son figured out exactly what to say so I would help him buy a car.

"I've decided," he announced over the phone one day last month, "to buy a moped, so I have some way to get around."

A moped.

An itsy teensy motorbike. A method of transportation that leaves the rider completely vulnerable to those drivers whose mothers already have helped them buy cars.

"This is a completely irrational reaction," I said by way of introducing my response to his announcement. Then I began to cry.

The next day, I started shopping for a used car for Joel. I found a good deal—a great deal, really—and called him to tell him.

He was furious.

Why was I surprised? Why had I thought he would dance on the rooftop of his college dorm at the prospect of a car, especially a car his mother intended to help him buy?

Silly me.

He ranted. He railed. He refused to agree that the car I'd found was a good deal.

Calmly, I answered his arguments point for point. Less calmly, I told him he was being bullheaded. Totally out of control, I threw an Irish fit and then hung up before Joel could get in the last word.

A colleague who had overheard my side of the conversation remarked, "I don't know that I'd spend any more time trying to talk him into taking my money."

I decided that Don was right. Later that evening, I called Joel to apologize.

"I'm intruding in a situation you are capable of handling yourself," I said. "I withdraw my offer, and I know you'll solve this on your own."

He was surprised, but gracious.

This was not our first Car Crisis. That was over the Suzuki Sidekick, a little round Jeep-like vehicle.

I bought it for me, but I taught Joel to drive it—it was a stick shift. We both enjoyed the car.

Then one day he skidded on a patch of ice and collided with a telephone pole. He wasn't hurt, but as I stood looking at the damaged car, I was shocked at how tiny, how insubstantial, it suddenly appeared. I got it fixed and made plans to sell it.

Joel was heartbroken. He begged me to keep the car. He even offered to buy it from me, paying twenty-five dollars a week for the rest of my life. I said no.

Next, he chided me for turning into an old lady. Then he appealed to my sense of adventure. He even attempted to tap into the only kind of guilt I do—Mother Guilt. But I carried through with my plan, and sold the car.

Not an hour went by during the next year that Joel didn't bring up the Sidekick and my betrayal of both it and him. Sometimes I responded; sometimes I hid in my room so I didn't have to hear it.

When he graduated from high school, Joel announced he needed a car. When he left for college, he restated his position. At Christmas, he was disappointed not to find a car in his stack of presents.

Then, last month, he called up and announced he was planning to buy a moped. You know the rest.

What you don't know is that he came home the next weekend and went to look at the very car I had found for him. He politely asked if I would help him buy it, and I politely said I would put some money down on it, but he would be in charge of the monthly payments.

Joel drove his first car back to college the next day.

"What's next?" I asked some older, more experienced parents at the office.

One man looked at me and smiled.

"Next," he said, "he'll get married and want a house."
May 14, 1993

Joel Goes to Europe

I didn't get long, contemplative letters from my son this summer, but I did get short, contemplative messages from him on my answering machine.

Frankly, that's better than I expected in the way of personal communication from a twenty-year-old on the loose in Europe.

Maybe "loose" isn't the right word. For the first two months, he was studying engineering in Nancy, France, but he spent long weekends in Prague, in Amsterdam, in Luxembourg. Then for two weeks, he was definitely on the loose, traveling with friends in Switzerland, Germany, Italy and Austria.

Joel kept me up to date with those phone messages, personal news bulletins I came to anticipate eagerly.

My favorite was recorded on July 13: "Mom, I'm in Paris, in the Place de Bastille. It's 2 a.m., the day before Bastille Day, and everybody is partying!"

Another that delighted me was this: "Mom, I'm in Rome. It's great! Let's see—I won seventy dollars at a casino in Monte Carlo a few nights ago. I left right away so I wouldn't lose the money I'd won. And I've got these spots on my hands from swimming with jellyfish, but I think they'll go away."

We did actually speak to each other from time to time, but most often, Joel called me at home when I was at work or at work when I was at home. Hence the many messages.

Joel called his dad when his clothes were stolen out of the car in Amsterdam. Apparently, thugs popped the trunk and sorted through the students' duffel bags. Joel reported losing some shoes, a pair of green corduroy pants, a couple of T-shirts and most of his boxer shorts.

Oh, yes—his compact disc player also was stolen.

The last thing I said to him at the airport when he left was this: "Have a wonderful time, remember I love you and know that someone is going to steal your CD player."

I'm sure Joel called his dad instead of me because he was afraid I'd say "Come home immediately" or worse, "I told you so."

One day, just before his classes ended, Joel left a message saying that he was sick. I called his school.

I speak French learned at Webster Groves High School thirty years ago, which means I do not speak it well enough to speak it aloud. When I do speak it aloud, I stick to short sentences, just the pertinent subject and a verb, always in the present tense.

When I got the school, I managed to say hello in French, but I switched to English when I asked to talk to Joel. The woman on the phone replied that she didn't speak English.

I said Joel's name again. Then, en français, I said that I was his mother. Then I said, "Il est mal," which I thought meant "He is sick."

Later, I learned that what I actually had said was: "He is bad."

The woman asked me to call back in ten minutes. In that time, I called the man here who serves as my personal French-language expert, and he helped me craft some simple sentences. I didn't need them, as the man I spoke to at the school spoke English.

By the time Joel and I got to talk to each other, he had visited a doctor and was much better.

The phone message that particularly touched me was this: "Mom, I'm in Vienna. I've lost my wallet. (Pause.) I guess it was dumb to call you, because you can't do anything about it."

Just a few hours later, I found a second message: "Mom, I took care of it. I talked to the police and to the embassy. I canceled my credit card. I talked to Dad, and he wired me money. I've got my passport and airplane ticket, so I'm still coming home."

Even though he got sick, and even though he lost his CD player, his underwear and his wallet, apparently Joel gained a great deal.

August 19, 1995

Perfectly Suited

My son has reached another milestone, experienced another "first" in his life. It's not exactly material for his baby book, which is just as well, as I've fallen behind in making regular entries, but it is significant nonetheless.

I'm not talking about his twenty-first birthday, which was three weeks ago. No, this is more important than even that.

He bought a suit.

Joel, a junior in college, called one day and said he had had several good interviews with corporations looking for students for work-study programs and summer internships. He is majoring in general engineering and business, with a minor in French. Still, he's not totally corporate—he recently auditioned for a campus production of *Hair*.

I congratulated him on his interviews. Then I asked a pointed question.

"What shoes did you wear?" I said.

"Well, I don't exactly have the right shoes—I wore my Doc Martens—but they seemed to like me anyway," he said.

I said I'd send him money for grown-up shoes.

A few days later, Joel called to say one of the companies wanted to fly him to their corporate headquarters for another round of interviews.

"I think I need a suit," he said. He paused. "What exactly is a suit?"

I explained suits, as best I understand them: jackets and pants that match, worn with a nice tie and a long-sleeved shirt that has been ironed.

Not that I had to explain ironing to Joel.

He irons. I don't. Never have. Well, hardly ever. The Halloween that he was just four, Joel came down the basement early in the afternoon and found me ironing part of the costume I planned to wear that night.

Joel had never seen the ironing board in use, as I used it then (and I use it now) as a storage shelf. Astonished, he looked at the ironing board and the iron and said, "What is all this? What are you doing?"

I've always answered Joel's questions as honestly as possible, and I tried to explain ironing to him.

I said that, really, except on the occasional Halloween, no one ever needed to iron. As long as you grab the clothes out of the dryer before it stops and you shake them vigorously, you simply don't need to iron.

I said if you had some article of clothing that absolutely required ironing (and that would be a gift item, as you would never buy such an article of clothing), then you took it to the dry cleaner, and they ironed it for you.

This was, of course, long before the wrinkled look came into fashion. Today, you don't even have to iron things that some people used to think had to be ironed.

In spite of my wise counsel, Joel grew up to be someone who irons. He taught himself how when he was in high school. One day, during his sophomore year, he came up from the basement and asked if I would buy him an iron.

"What's wrong with the iron we have?" I asked.

"Mom," he said, "the iron we have is the one you got as a wedding present twenty-two years ago, and it's held together with masking tape. I want a new iron."

We went shopping that very day.

Back to the suit. Joel said a lot of other students wore suits to interviews, and he thought he'd better get one for this appointment.

Big-boy clothes! First, big-boy shoes, and now a real suit, all in the course of a few days.

As he talked, my mind raced through a lot of other "firsts" in his life, precious memories of his childhood. However, as the mother of a man, I refrained from saying what I was thinking.

What I did say was this: "Try to get a suit that's on sale, and try to get one that doesn't make you look like a Young Republican."

November 4, 1995

Happy Father's Day

A friend was spinning tales of another woman's troubles with her teen-ager.

"You know what it's like," he said, summing up a litany of the woman's frustration. "You're a single parent."

A moment or two passed before I spoke. My reply surprised and pleased me at the same time.

"No, I'm not," I said. "I've been divorced for sixteen years, but I have never been a single parent."

Joel's dad and I split up almost sixteen years ago, when our son was six. We petitioned the court for joint custody, an uncommon request at the time. We said on paper that we would share equally the expenses and the caretaking of our little boy. We meant what we said, though I think now neither of us knew exactly how it would go.

What we knew for certain was that we both needed our little boy in the center of our lives. Neither of us was willing to give up watching him grow, and we convinced ourselves that we could remain a family of sorts even though we lived apart. That sounds reasonable by today's standards, but in 1980, it was a radical notion. In most "broken homes," as they were called, the mother kept the children and the father visited them from time to time—or not.

The lawyer we hired to dissolve our eleven-year marriage congratulated us on our decision but said she hoped we wouldn't be in her office every few months, fighting over whose turn it was to buy a winter coat or a red wagon or new tennis shoes. She said that was common when divorced parents shared custody.

That never happened.

What did happen was that by fits and starts, in spite of hurt feelings and angry outbursts on both sides, we learned together how to be good parents even though we no longer were married.

It wasn't easy, especially at first. Still, we both worked hard to speak to each other in civil, if not quite courteous, tones. We restricted our conversations to matters concerning Joel and his schedule or his needs. Over time, we've become downright cordial and expanded considerably our range of topics.

We didn't speak ill of each other to Joel. We did agree to continue to live in the same school district, so as not to introduce another major change in his life. We each set up a fully furnished bedroom for him in our respective homes, and we divided his time equally between us in the course of each week. That seemed awkward at first, but it allowed each of us to be a full-time parent part of the time, rather than assigning one of us the role of "visiting" parent.

We didn't play games with Joel's schedule, keeping him too long some days or dropping him off too early other days. We didn't ever begrudge each other time spent with him, or try to compete with extra presents on his birthday or at Christmas.

We practiced patience—and made the round-trip drive—when he left his blue sweater or his English book at the "other" house. We each took Joel on modest family vacations. His father also took him camping, and I took him to the theater. We made sure that both of us spent time with him every holiday, no matter what the regular schedule.

Most important, perhaps, was that we presented a united front through the years.

When Joel tried to wiggle out of dinner at my house because he didn't care for the menu on a given night, his dad told him he would have to make the best of it. When the after-school sitter's son taught our son to shoplift, we both came down hard, saying that was unacceptable behavior. When we had to make occasional, unpopular decisions as Joel got older, we consulted by phone, made the decisions together.

When Joel's dad married a wonderful woman a few years after our divorce, I encouraged them to let Joel participate in the wedding. All three of us paced the floor at the hospital during Joel's emergency appendectomy, and then we worked out a schedule so one of us was there with him around the clock.

All three of us went to school conferences and open houses. We sat together and cheered at the football games when Joel was on the freshman team. We sat together and applauded when Joel appeared in school plays. We all went along, our cars packed full, when Joel left for college.

We've told him all along (and tell him still) how lucky he was to have three parents to love him.

We've never kept records of who spent what, never tried to quantify our parenting to make sure it was absolutely equal, but I think we both tried to give 100 percent. Our goal was to keep our child as close to our hearts as he was the day he was born. We worked hard to bring him up to be a good and kind man with strong values and a life full of love and laughter.

We succeeded, and we did so while living apart.

Happy Father's Day, Tom—and thanks.

June 15, 1996

Buddies in Dayton

Earlier this month, I went to Dayton, Ohio, to visit an office cubicle.

Actually, I went to visit my son, who is working in Dayton this summer. But the specific invitation that he extended was this: "I want you to come see my cubicle."

That was my first clue that this was to be a visit between adults, regardless of our relationship. After all, adults, not children, have cubicles in office buildings.

The workspace itself is not so remarkable, of course, but what it represents in Joel's life is important. He is twenty-one, and will be a senior in college this fall. This summer job is his first brush with corporate life, and it is very much an adult experience.

When Joel picked me up at the airport, I was wearing the one grown-up-lady dress I had brought along. Also, I had replaced my jade green nail polish with a tasteful rose color. Obviously, I passed inspection, as he suggested we head directly to his office for a tour.

I wish I could explain what it is he does in his cubicle. With my limited grasp of the industry that fascinates him, I call it "computer stuff." It's not coding or programming, he says. It's telecommunications engineering. Like I said, computer stuff.

After the visit to the cubicle, we occupied ourselves for three days with activities we enjoy.

We headed for the mall one morning, where I spent the motel money on some new work clothes for Joel. "Motel money" amounted to what I was saving by staying in Joel's apartment. Since he had extended his hospitality, it seemed only fair to pass along what I would have paid for a room elsewhere.

One morning, we drove to the Cincinnati Zoo and Botanical Garden, about a thirty-minute drive from Dayton. There, we toured the brand-new Wings of the World exhibit, delighting in the variety of birds we saw. We trekked through the Jungle Trails exhibit, which simulates rainforests in both Asia and Africa. And we talked to the elephants—something we do whenever we have the privilege of being in the company of elephants.

Joel toured the insect exhibit. Together, we admired the three baby walruses. We laughed at the clever primates. And we especially enjoyed standing high up in the bald eagles' aerie.

Across the river from Cincinnati, in Covington, Kentucky, we boarded a boat and went for an hour-long cruise. Back in Dayton, we visited a park along the river. We stopped at an exhibit of an Indian reservation. We ate several good meals, sometimes with a glass of wine.

We didn't really do anything we haven't done before, but somehow, we did it all differently—as friends, rather than as mother and son. The entire time we were together, there was only one incident of childishness, and that was when I said I was afraid to go see the movie *Independence Day* because movie aliens scare me.

Even on that matter, we compromised, and went to a

matinee so I would have plenty of daylight hours to get over being scared.

We also rented some movies, watching *The American President* and *Get Shorty* together. And for old times' sake, we sat and watched an episode of "Star Trek: Deep Space Nine."

As I recall, there was one moment when my inherent motherliness erupted all over the kitchen. In a matter of moments, I unloaded the clean dishes from the dishwasher, filled it back up with dirty dishes, wiped off the counter and then started a load of laundry, for good measure.

Joel politely pointed out that I need not do any housework, so I stopped.

We did have some wonderful conversations, about matters grand and trivial. We laughed a lot. And we talked about what's next for Joel.

The company where he works has already offered him a job after he graduates. He asked me what I thought about that, considering that he would like to get a graduate degree before entering the workforce.

I told him to go slowly. I also told him that men tend to use the same language at work that they use in relationships. Say how much you enjoy working there, I said. Tell them you are learning a great deal and that you really appreciate the opportunity to be there.

Then, I said, say you are not ready to make a commitment.

I'm convinced that lots of companies will be interested in hiring Joel, both after he graduates next spring and after he earns a graduate degree.

He may have just a cubicle today, but someday soon, this young man is going to have a great big office.

July 27, 1996

Cheerleader for Life

Mother as Private Secretary, Mother as Short-order Cook, Mother as last-resort Movie Date. Sound familiar? Your kids must have been home from college, too. My son enjoyed a month-long break from the rigors of engineering classes and I found that I was busier than ever. The phone never stopped ringing. "Hi, this is George. Is Joel there?" "Hi, it's Ellen. Is Joel home?" "Hi, this is G. Is Joel up yet?"

No, no and no (especially if it was before 3 p.m.).

After two unsuccessful attempts to see *The Crucible* with friends—the show was sold out both times—Joel made it to the movie when a friend and I bought the tickets in advance. Back home at 9 p.m., Joel was in the mood for macaroni and cheese, a snack to hold him until 11:30 p.m., when he went out with friends.

Of course it was good to have him home. It's just that I'm not used to playing all these roles anymore. Joel is twenty-two, and at this point I usually serve in one capacity only: Mother as Cheerleader.

On the phone, in e-mail and in those rare moments when I see him during a weekend visit home from school, here is what I say: "Good for you! I'm proud of you! You made a good decision! Congratulations on winning that honor! I'm so happy for you! Wow, that's great news!" and on and on, without benefit of pompons.

He's smart, he's focused, he's ambitious, and he has far outdistanced me academically. And so, my duties in the one job I take more seriously than any other—that of being a mother—have shrunk to just this one task, that of being a cheerleader. I'm good at it. My pride is genuine.

Imagine my surprise when I discovered that he is not yet ready to serve as cheerleader for me.

We always argue during the holidays; it's inevitable. (Surely you didn't think that happens only in your house.) This year, we lived mostly in harmony until December 31, when Joel picked up a travel brochure lying on the coffee table. This is what he read:

"You are invited on a journey in awakenings of the heart as we follow Egypt's ancient paths of initiation. The word 'Egypt' alone stimulates feelings of mystery, power and heightened awareness. We are stirred by the ancients as we explore several of the earth's most sacred sites: The Great Pyramid, the Sphinx, the Temples of the Nile. We attune to the energies of Egypt, fully conscious of her magic, adventure and wisdom."

Joel was unimpressed. He went so far as to intimate that if I were interested in such a tour, I was crazy.

Being thought of as crazy does not offend me. Usually I am called that when exploring unfamiliar beliefs or practices. For instance, I got a letter recently from a reader who pronounced me "wacko" because I had written about Feng Shui, the ancient Chinese art of placement.

I enjoy learning what other people believe and why. It's an ecumenical approach to life, in the largest sense of the word. I credit my fallen-away-Catholic father and my fallen-away-Baptist mother for teaching me this approach. Also, my aunt saw to it that I was christened in a Catholic church and my maternal grandmother arranged for me to be saved at a Baptist revival some years later, so I started out exceptionally well versed, religiously speaking.

Growing up, I was encouraged to attend churches of different denominations. I did that from time to time, and I learned that what seems most important is not what faith you call your own but how you treat other people in the course of your life. As an adult, reading about Hinduism, Buddhism and other "isms" confirmed that view for me in a more universal sense.

What harm is there, I said to Joel, in learning about the lives and beliefs of the ancient Egyptians? And isn't it to be expected, I said, that we would have different interests? He thinks sky-diving is cool; I want to swim with sperm whales. He's into exotic beer; Irish whiskey makes me frisky. He likes thought-provoking drama; I am particularly fond of musicals.

At twenty-two, he's asking "Who am I?" At forty-eight, I'm asking "Why am I here?" He's beginning to define himself by figuring out what he isn't. I'm beginning to figure out where I fit in the grand scheme of things, and how to live accordingly. He's a scientist, and I'm something of a modern-day mystic. Even Carl Sagan, a scientist of considerable stature, said there is room for more in life than science.

Reporting on our argument to a friend, I whined that I wished Joel could be more supportive. She pointed out that he has always been protective of me, and that might be the role he's playing now.

So as we barrel ahead into 1997, the report from here is we've got Mother as Cheerleader and Son as Guard. Ah, sweet sport.

February 8, 1997

The Beginning of the End

In August of 1993, when my son first headed off to college, I wrote him a letter filled with free, but heartfelt, advice.

I published that letter in a column, and every August since

then, readers with children leaving for college have called to ask me to reprint the column. I have done that, and I promise I'll run it again this year.

Just now, though, I need to write a letter to my discombobulated self.

Dear Self,

After six years at college, Joel has earned a master's degree. He also has accepted a job in Palo Alto, California. It's a good job, work he's looking forward to at a good company in a beautiful part of the country.

Isn't this wonderful?

Absolutely, and I am very proud. I also am sad.

Not all the time. Most of the time, I'm excited and completely delighted for him. But from time to time, my thoughts take a different turn.

For instance: I think about how far California is from home. Joel will no longer have the lengthy vacations that have allowed him to spend time with the family for the past six years. Of course, I'll go visit him, but probably not very often, just because of the distance and the expense.

Besides, he is busy making a new life for himself, and I don't want to be a pest.

Well, maybe I do, but I must try not to be.

All this makes me sad, and I miss Joel already, even though as I write this, he's not yet left for California.

There is always joy, even amid sadness, when you discover you are not alone. At Joel's graduation, I met another mother and son. She lives near Chicago. He has taken a job in Minneapolis.

"I've been crying a lot," she confided. "I know this is a great opportunity for him, and I'm very proud, but I will miss him so much."

Some of this, I suspect, is about missing our sons, and

some of it is acknowledgment that graduation from college is a huge transition for parents as well as students.

No wonder schools call the graduation ceremony "commencement." If they told the whole truth, they would have to give the nod to the endings taking place at the same time as the beginnings.

Graduation from college, after all, is the beginning of life in the adult world, the "real" world, as those of us not ensconced in academia call it. That means, of course, that we parents are in for another gigantic shift in our roles, one that began the day we took our children to kindergarten and ends the day we hug those children, now adults taller than we are, as they stand before us triumphant in caps and gowns on a college campus.

Of course, this transition doesn't mean there will be no more good times with Joel. In fact, we spent some time together on a recent weekend, doing things we enjoy doing together, things we're good at. We went to the Zoo, and we were lucky enough to watch a keeper feed the bears an afternoon snack.

Later, back at home, we ordered a pizza. And we watched a nature video together.

The video talked a lot about bonding between mother animals and their offspring.

"Mothering is addictive," the announcer intoned at one point. Bonding, he said, causes beta endorphins to be released in both the mother and the child, and these endorphins are as powerful as morphine.

Joel and I looked at each other and laughed. "Maybe that's my problem," I said. "I'm addicted to mothering."

As long as we were spending a nature-filled day, I really wanted to mention, just in passing, that male orcas never leave their mothers. The female whales are the matriarchs of the pod, and their sons stay with them for life.

I didn't bring it up, only because I knew Joel would have pointed out that we are not now and never have been orcas.

Still, it's nice to know some sons stick around. Mine, however, has opted to take advantage of the wider world, the world I helped introduce him to by taking him on trips when he was younger.

And that's a good thing, or it will be, as soon as I get used to it.

Maybe I need to concentrate on the part I played, with a lot of help from Joel's dad and his other mother, in Joel's success.

Good for us—all of us. Now buck up.

May 29, 1999

This Is My Saab Story

"This is my Saab story."

That's what Lindsay said in a conversation about the cars. It was such a good line that I've swiped it and used it again at the end of this column.

The occasion was a forty-eight-hour obsession over Saab convertibles. This wasn't my obsession. On vacation in California, I watched my son, Joel, move from a mild interest to a roaring preoccupation with the cars. Sometimes, a topic comes to mind that just pushes everything else aside, and fortunately, we had the time to indulge it.

As I recall, it started slowly. On the way to the beach from his home in Menlo Park, Joel started talking cars. This was unusual, as he drives an ancient Mazda that he has sworn never to part with. At first, he approached the topic tentatively, but within a short time, he was pointing out Saab convertibles on the road. That was easy, because they are everywhere on the road in northern California. And why not? The weather is beautiful every day, perfect for a convertible.

Later, relaxing back at home, I opened a new issue of *Gourmet*. Right behind the cover was a double-truck ad for the Saab convertible. "It's a sign," I said, laughing, and pushed the ad across the table toward Joel. While he looked at it, I perused the ads for used cars in the local paper. There was a '95 Saab for sale with everything Joel wanted except standard transmission. One thing led to another, and soon we were in Palo Alto, looking at the car, which was a gorgeous burgundy color.

The next day, everything heated up. I remembered that my friend Richard had a Saab, and the Saab always had the final vote on whether Richard went where he planned to go—it was a most unreliable car. Still, that was years ago. We got online and looked at Saab repair records. Apparently, that is no longer an issue.

The money might be an issue. A new Saab convertible costs about $40,000.

"Lease one," I said. Not that I've ever done that, but I know people who have. They drive splendid, expensive cars because leasing costs less than buying. Joel was appalled. He insisted that owning is better than leasing. I reminded him that he rents part of a house because no one but royalty can buy a house in Silicon Valley. Just about then, one of the other guys who lives in the house came along and joined the conversation. As it happens, Jim leases his car.

One thing, once again, led to another, and suddenly the three of us were in Jim's car, buzzing along the highway to a Saab dealer. We meandered around the lot, looking at used Saab convertibles. A salesman popped out the door, and in a few minutes, there we were, cruising along in one of the cars. At Jim's suggestion, before we left the dealership, Joel sat down to discuss the ins and outs of leasing.

I went to the parts department and bought Joel a T-shirt with a Saab convertible on it, figuring that was the most help I could be on this project.

As we pulled back in at Joel's, he spied a Saab convertible in a neighbor's driveway and went over for some car talk. Back at home, we got online again. We looked at other convertibles. Most of them cost slightly more than half what the Saab costs. Joel didn't care for the looks of those cars. Then there is the Rolls-Royce Corniche, which goes for almost ten times more than the Saab. He ruled that out, too. We looked at lists of used Saabs for sale in the area. We looked at lists of inventory that local Saab dealers had on the lots, both new and used. We looked up tips on how to get a good lease. We even took an online quiz to determine whether Joel was a good candidate for a lease.

"Just do it," said Jim, but Joel isn't the "just do it" type.

That evening, we talked about Saabs again over dinner with Jim and Joel's friend Lindsay. At one point, Joel blurted out that he had noticed my less-than-enthusiastic response during the test drive. "Don't you like the car?" he asked.

I remembered the sporty car with its clean lines. I remembered the exhilarating experience of the wind rushing through my hair. But I also remembered the winding mountain roads on the way to the beach, and I remembered that there is no roll bar on the Saab convertible. (For that matter, there is no roll bar on any convertibles anymore.)

"I like the car," I said. "I like the car a lot, and it would be lots of fun to have one. But as a mother, I am concerned about your safety. When you drive it, would you consider wearing a helmet?"

And that's my Saab story.

July 29, 2000

A RIP IN THE SPACE SUIT

In September of 1993, I was diagnosed with breast cancer. The surgeon told me just moments after the biopsy that I had cancer, and in my ignorance, I assumed I would be dead within the week. Now I know there are two million breast cancer survivors in the United States, and every day I am delighted to be one of them.

Breast cancer is at epidemic proportions, and the sisterhood, as it were, grows every day. I take great comfort in being friends with women who were diagnosed five years, ten years, even twenty years ago, and for that reason I have included these columns in this book. When you meet someone or read about someone who has been through breast cancer, you begin to believe that you, too, will make it.

That's my advice for anyone newly diagnosed—find yourself a bosom buddy.

Breast Cancer Awareness

October is National Breast Cancer Awareness Month, and boy, am I aware.

I had read that 1,600,000 women in the United States have been diagnosed with breast cancer and that another million women have it but don't yet know it.

I had read that one in eight women will get breast cancer.

I had read that every eleven minutes, a woman dies of breast cancer; that the disease is the leading cause of cancer death in women ages fifteen to fifty-two.

I had read that breast cancer research is sorely under-funded though no one yet knows how to prevent or cure the disease.

I was well informed, or so I thought.

Then I was diagnosed with breast cancer. On September 20, I had a biopsy of a lump I found late in May. It was cancer. On September 26, I had a lumpectomy—the centimeter-sized tumor and some surrounding tissue were removed—and I also had several lymph nodes removed from under my arm. On October 2, I learned that one lymph node was cancerous. I began a short course of chemotherapy on October 12, and I will have radiation treatments early next year.

I know a lot more now than I did, say, on September 19, and it's unlikely that I'll think about the disease now only during National Breast Cancer Awareness Month.

My first inclination was to tell everyone I knew; to go through my address book and spread the word. Why? Because I do not want to go through this alone. I knew I needed help. I asked for it. And I got it, beyond anything I ever expected.

That first night, just hours after the biopsy, close friends started showing up at the door with hugs and flowers. In the course of the evening, I finally reached my son, who is away at school. We talked for a while, and then he asked about the voices in the background.

"Well," I said, "people are coming over."

"You're having an 'I Have Cancer' party?" Joel asked.

"Yes. Exactly that."

The friend who had volunteered to cook anything I wanted that night ended up making garlic mashed potatoes for the whole crowd, served with almond M&Ms. (The blue ones were particularly popular.)

My second inclination was to read everything I could find on the disease. I read about the stages of breast cancer, the treatments for breast cancer, the survival rates for breast cancer. I read worst-case scenarios and stories of personal triumph. After just two hours of this, my whole body was trembling.

I mentioned aloud my sudden aversion to cold, hard facts, and my friends immediately swept through the house, removing every book that contained the word "breast" except the dictionary. Since then, I have learned to read selectively—and in small doses—about specific aspects of breast cancer that relate to my experience.

Also, I have taken to heart advice shared by Joyce Wadler in her wonderful (and unscary) book *My Breast: One Woman's Cancer Story*. To wit: I now control how much information goes out and how much comes in, depending on who is asking and who is telling.

Right now, I'm putting into practice a personal healing program that includes Western medicine, frequent naps, Eastern philosophy, assorted vitamins, Native American spiritualism, moderate exercise and occasional flights of neo-Druid fancy.

I've spent some time afraid, but it's impossible to sweep up debris that accumulates in the future, so I put away the broom. I've spent some time wary of my body, but decided it's imperative to go back to loving it for its strength and beauty. And I've spent some time laughing—lots of funny things happen when you get cancer.

I'm feeling lucky—it was tiny, we got it early, it was in just one node. Also, I'm feeling loved, buoyed up daily by friends who cook for me, drive me to appointments, pray for me and make me laugh and by readers who send me notes and cards expressing support and encouragement.

One friend, Wendy Reid Crisp, an author and the former editor of *Sassy* magazine, told me a story recently that expresses perfectly what life is like for me just now.

Two years ago, her hometown had three devastating earthquakes within eighteen hours. Much of the town just fell down. Wendy's friend Pam called to say that another friend's house had collapsed. Nancy (the woman who lost the house) and Pam went to the Red Cross station at the fairgrounds to see what they could do to help.

Once there, Pam suddenly said, "Nancy, take a sandwich. We're the victims here. We don't always have to be the ones who make the sandwiches. Sometimes, we have to be the ones to take the sandwiches."

I'm taking sandwiches. Thanks for making them.
October 28, 1995

Han Solo Had the Right Idea

How do you get breast cancer?

No one knows for sure, but there are many possibilities, ranging from the absurd to the highly likely. Living with a life-threatening disease offers physical and emotional challenges, to be sure, but perhaps most taxing are the intellectual gymnastics required to figure out how it happened.

OK, maybe "required" isn't the right word, but I've found it impossible not to wonder. Here are just some of the options, culled from way too much reading.

1. EMFs. (Not to be confused with Ents, those enchanting tree-beings in the Tolkien Trilogy.) Some scientists say electromagnetic fields—the bad vibes from microwaves, televisions, computers, cellular phones, utility poles and waterbed heaters—cause cancer.

2. Water. Some scientists say our water supply is to blame, because of agricultural and industrial runoff upstream in our rivers. Think bottled water from now on.

3. Slumbering Immune System. Some scientists say chemotherapy and radiation are ineffective treatments against cancer and should be obsolete, that we should be jumpstarting the slumbering immune system that allowed cancer to take hold.

I asked my oncologist about this. He pointed out that people who say that don't say how to jumpstart the immune system—science hasn't figured out how.

4. Hormones. Breast cancer is common in females and uncommon in males, so scientists say that hormones may play a big part in the disease. In other words, you may be at risk simply because you have breasts.

5. Underwear. No, really. One theory goes that wearing tight bras too much of the time restricts blood flow and may cause cancer. Just to be sure, I say we cut back to three days a week, and only between 9 a.m. and 5 p.m. on those days.

6. Diet. Some scientists say a high-fat, low-fiber diet causes cancer. Eating right always makes sense, of course, but what if you switch to strictly broccoli and tofu and then they find out that it was the EMFs all along?

7. Suppressed Anguish. A cancer specialist in Houston insists that suppressing anguish over tragedies in your past causes cancer in your present. So it's your fault, you anguish-suppressor you.

The night I had an Irish fit over the Houston specialist's book (much wailing, gnashing of teeth and occasional outbursts of profanity), my friend Edward grabbed the book out of my hand, opened my front door and threw the book in the street. Then he went out and drove over it until the book could do me—or anyone else—no harm.

8. Genes. Maybe your mother or your aunt had breast cancer, but even if they didn't, you may not be safe. One in eight women alive today may develop breast cancer, and more and more new cases are occurring in women with no family history.

9. Karma. Spiritually speaking, maybe this was your lifetime to learn to live with breast cancer. Certainly, the side effects of common cancer treatments take away much that you might be vain about (pretty hair, soft skin, high energy), so the spiritual aspects of the disease are hard to overlook.

10. Stress. Too many places to go, people to see, things to do may lead to cancer. But how many are too many?

Overall, the "how" game is less fraught with agony than the "WHAT IF" game, which always is played in upper case letters, as in WHAT IF IT COMES BACK? WHAT IF I CAN'T

Another frightening exercise is trying to relate a life you're quite fond of to national statistics. On this matter, I've sided with Han Solo of *Star Wars* fame. When C3PO recited the statistical probability of successfully maneuvering through an asteroid field while Solo was trying to do just that, Solo snapped, "Never tell me the odds."

Perhaps the only head game worth playing when confronting breast cancer is answering this question: What can I learn from this?

January 6, 1996

Repairing a Rip in the Space Suit

My friend Elizabeth refers to her body as her space suit, a garment necessary while visiting Earth. When she developed a health problem last year, she called to say her space suit was torn and she was having it fixed.

Six months ago, I wrote here that I had been diagnosed in September with breast cancer—a rip, if you will, in my space suit. In response to dozens of inquiries, I am writing today to say the rip has been mended.

I've finished four rounds of chemotherapy and thirty-three radiation-therapy treatments. I make time now for such therapies as massage, exercise and regular attendance at a support group. Preventive measures—chemical, physical and spiritual—also are part of my healing.

And I have about an inch of slate-gray hair on my head

that sticks up in such a way that one friend has taken to calling me Baby Huey.

When he calls me that, I laugh.

I've laughed at least twice as often as I've cried since September. Once I learned that breast cancer—any kind of cancer, actually—is not an automatic death sentence, I took a deep breath and started to think again about living. Once I quit reading about the disease and started reading about surviving it, fear receded. Soon after, joy rebounded.

I didn't do this by myself. I've had support from:

* Family and friends
* Caring doctors and other medical professionals
* My cozy overstuffed couch, site of a daily late-afternoon nap
* The Wellness Community

A word is in order about the latter. The Wellness Community is a support center for people with cancer and their families and friends. There are fourteen in the country. The centers sponsor educational workshops, stress-reducing programs and weekly support groups—all free.

One evening a week, I spend two hours there with strangers who quickly have become trusted confidants. These are the people who nod in assent when I speak, not just because they are sympathetic or polite, but because they understand what it is like to have cancer.

For instance, when I confessed that I was overwhelmed by the abundance of information on alternative treatment options, in turn they told me how they handled that. Then, one dear woman cautioned me against trying to be a "perfect cancer patient."

No wonder the services are free. How could you put a price on the reassurance that you are not alone?

At home, too, there are potent reminders that I have lots

of help learning to survive breast cancer. Taped to the bathroom mirror are these words, scrawled by a friend on a piece of notebook paper: "For today, I am only going to think about today."

In mid-March, when I invited over some of the people who look after me (it may take a village to raise a child, but it took more than forty people to get me through the first three weeks of breast cancer), some wag used my eyebrow pencil (had to be a man; a woman knows how hard it is to get just the right point on an eyebrow pencil) to add this to the note: ". . . unless there is something really fun going on tomorrow."

One thing that certainly is going on "tomorrow" is that I hope to use some of what I'm learning to help others who have heard their surgeons say, "It's cancer." I'm not sure yet what form that help will take, as I'm still new at this myself.

People ask if I'm my old self now that the medical treatments are over. In short, no. But I've decided that I don't want to be my old self, even when all my energy is back. I intend to be a new self.

I think now that I was living too fast, too busy doing instead of being. I was taking too much for granted. I was confusing trivial matters with important issues. These all are lessons that I thought I had learned, but I see now that I was not living accordingly.

How fortunate I am to have a space suit that mended relatively easily, and to get a second chance.

April 6, 1996

One Year Later

One year ago, I learned I had breast cancer.

On the day of the biopsy, the surgeon stitched me up and then told me in the operating room that the lump was cancerous. He sounded very far away. My first thought was how awkward it was for me to have to hear this news in the company of strangers. Then I realized that all five people in the room were gathered around the table, holding my hands and stroking my forehead, my arms and my legs.

My second thought was how awkward it must be for these good people to have to deliver this terrifying message, day after day. Finally, I quit thinking and began listening as my doctor explained my options. My attention wandered only twice: once when my leg started shaking uncontrollably and again when I realized I would have to tell this news, say aloud that I had cancer, to my son, who was away at college.

A nurse wheeled me to an outpatient recovery room, where my friend waited. The nurse left us alone for a minute. With amazement in my voice, I said, "It's cancer."

Barb shook her head and said, "No." I told her again. She said, "No, don't say that." She started to cry, I started to cry, and we held each other. When she called her husband to tell him, he was so upset that he wouldn't talk.

One year ago, I thought if you got cancer—any kind—you automatically died soon after. I didn't know then that there are more than 100 different kinds of cancers, many of them highly treatable. I didn't know then that there are eight million cancer survivors in America. I didn't know then that many people undergoing chemotherapy or radiation treatments continued to work, to play, to live and to love.

I spent some misguided moments thinking I would never again travel. Yet in April, one month after all my cancer treatments were over, I went to Los Angeles to spend a week sitting on the beach, staring at the Pacific Ocean. In June, I went to New York City to see four plays in three days. In July, I spent a week relaxing in rural Missouri.

One year ago, I was not at all certain that my naturally curly hair would grow back after chemotherapy. It fell out on October 28, a difficult day I will never forget. Less than one year later, I now have so much thick, curly hair that it actually needs to be cut—if I can bring myself to do that.

Seven months ago, I joined a weekly support group at the Wellness Community, an agency in Olivette that provides free services to people with cancer and their families. I met and shared stories with wonderful people, people working their way through the many changes that cancer causes in our lives. I stayed long enough to be helped and, I hope, to help. One month ago, I resigned from the group, confident that the skills I learned there will continue to serve me well.

Two weeks ago, I talked to Shirley Vogler Meister in Indianapolis. A published poet and newspaper columnist, Shirley's sister had a biopsy a few months ago on a lump that turned out to be benign. The frightening experience somehow caused Shirley to remember this silly verse she used to chant with other women in her exercise class: "The bust, the bust— we must develop the bust! The bigger the better, the tighter the sweater—the men depend on us."

Shirley has recently rewritten the silly exercise ditty this way: "The bust, the bust—we must remember the bust! Earlier tests put minds at rest—our lives depend on us."

One week ago, I took myself to the Sanibel Harbour Resort and Spa in Fort Myers, Florida. There, I signed up for two massages, a facial, an aromatic body wrap and other sybaritic treatments. Also, I walked on the beach. I watched pelicans fish. I introduced myself to a treecrab living high in the branches of a red mangrove. I made time for every sunset, from various vantage points—a pontoon boat, my balcony, a wicker rocker on the veranda of the hotel.

Being rubbed and wrapped rejuvenated me. The sight and sound of the water restored me. The opportunity to observe wildlife for hours at a time reminded me how little the corporate culture has to offer.

As I reviewed the past year, I reflected on the experience of having cancer. I made note of the changes I've made in my life. I acknowledged how grateful I am to be here, whole and happy. I thought about all that I still want to do, and I made a list of goals that will make each day more meaningful.

And then I put the cancer behind me, ready to move on.
September 28, 1996

New Beginnings

The tulips are up, the lilac bush has budded and I detect a sense of anticipation on the part of the ginkgo tree in my backyard. Spring, the season of new beginnings, is here.

One year ago this month, I had just completed four rounds of chemotherapy and thirty-three radiation treatments for breast cancer. The doctors had cautioned me that sometimes, people become depressed when treatments end, as you may no longer feel that you're actively fighting the disease. That didn't happen to me—I was delighted to stop focusing on something as scary as cancer.

What did happen is that I worried that A.B.C.—that's

After Breast Cancer, as opposed to B.B.C., Before Breast Cancer—I might launch my new life tentatively, with more fear than hope, figuratively holding my breath to see what would happen next. I worried that I might move lightly through life, as though walking on eggs.

I am delighted to report I've been making omelets, eggs Benedict, crabmeat quiches and scrambled eggs with fresh chives and feta cheese.

Looking back, I have no real sense of exactly when I once again began to embrace life fully. As anyone who has been through cancer treatments knows, you are profoundly tired much of the time. I spent that time being tired at work, tired at home and occasionally tired at the theater—and that was about it.

I do know it was the week before Thanksgiving, fully nine months after the treatments ended, that I woke up one morning and felt like myself again. Not the well-muscled, healthy self I had been prior to cancer, but a self finally ready to go back to the gym, a self able to walk farther than from here to the corner and a self willing to stay up—some nights, anyway—past 9 p.m.

Of course, I have directed some of my new-found energy into looking at the rest of my life, eager to make changes long overdue at work and in my personal life. I am in need of new beginnings, I told a friend.

That's how I came to run away to Egypt.

I heard about a two-week trip in the company of sixteen women from all over the country, guided by a fifth-generation Egyptologist. I didn't have the money, of course, but what does money matter when you've just beat cancer? I borrowed the money, and I went to Egypt because a year ago I couldn't, and now I could.

I knew before I left that scarab jewelry was popular, but I

never knew exactly why. While touring the tomb of Nefertari in the Valley of the Queens, I learned that the scarab is the symbol of new beginnings.

New beginnings! That's what I'm up to, even here in Egypt, I thought. I decided right then to buy a scarab souvenir of some sort.

I didn't have to.

After the tour, we headed back to our bus. The driver had brought along his eleven-year-old son, who sat across from me. Earlier in the day, I had noticed the boy watching me scan the sky with my binoculars, looking for birds. Before our group left the bus to tour the tombs, I had handed the binoculars to the boy and told him to enjoy himself. Upon my return, he thanked me and gave them back. Then, shyly, he placed something on the seat next to me. It was a small alabaster carving of a scarab.

"This is for you," he said.

Once home from Egypt, I enrolled in a belly dancing class. I've done all sorts of dancing in my life, and always wanted to try this. I figured it was B.Y.O.B. (Bring Your Own Belly), and as luck would have it, I'm equipped. After just one class, I realized I am learning something fun and getting a good workout at the same time. As time and budget allow, I may also take up the tin whistle.

I told my boss that, and he immediately suggested I combine the two.

"Do you know how few people belly dance and play the tin whistle at the same time? You could be a phenomenon," he said. When I stopped laughing, I agreed to perform one or the other—or maybe both, if I'm any good—at the office Christmas party.

Laughter, dance and music all are good for the soul—and for the cells.

Last year, I met a man named Tom at the Wellness Community who evaluates potentially stressful situations all day long by asking, "Is this good for my cells?"

If the answer is yes, he proceeds. If it's no, and Tom is caught up in momentary anger or fear or sadness, he stops and rethinks the situation. If he needs to say "no" and walk away, he does. If he needs to come around to a "yes" for the sake of moving on, he does.

Tom believes that his objective attention to his mental state practically guarantees a healthier body, from the cellular level on out.

Spring, I'm convinced, is good for everybody's cells. Here's to new beginnings at your house and mine!

March 22, 1997

A Day of Caring

When you've had breast cancer, sometimes you need to look into the sparkling eyes of another survivor, grab hands or maybe even hug, as a way of reminding each other "Hey, we're here. Life is good." Even survivors meeting for the first time feel the bond immediately and know what it took to get from there to here. We all are, as my friend Ina says, "bosom buddies," sisters in a universal sorority that we did not choose to join.

And so it was that I was hanging out backstage at the Khorassan Room of the Chase Park Plaza on April 7, talking with models preparing for a fashion show. The event was the Day of Caring, sponsored by the local chapter of AMC Cancer Research, a day for women touched in some way by breast cancer to come together to learn, laugh and eat lunch. About 700 people attended.

All eight models in the fashion show were breast cancer survivors, women who have made time in their full, busy lives for surgery, chemotherapy, radiation and recovery. In their daily lives, they are mothers, wives, political activists, meteorologists, volunteers, health educators and public relations specialists. Three of the women have had breast cancer twice. Three have helped care for mothers and sisters who also were diagnosed with the disease.

It was my privilege to speak about each woman before she headed down the runway. Their stories, summarized here, are unforgettable and of great value to anyone recently diagnosed.

* Geri Rothman-Serot was first diagnosed eighteen years ago. She experienced a recurrence eighteen months later. Geri donates time to charities, attends Jazzercise classes, goes to Rams games and speaks with women about breast cancer. She tells them that "fear is often what kills—not the disease." Geri also tells women that she is blessed to have survived cancer. "I enjoy my life so much more than people who haven't had it," she says.

* Joann Harris, diagnosed nine years ago, now works with a breast cancer outreach organization called Anna's Link, which targets the African-American community. Breast cancer changed her life, she says. "Since going through cancer, I am more positive. I tend to see good in everything and everybody. I don't have as much patience with people who complain all the time." Joann believes now that out of every lesson, there is a blessing.

* Debbie Davis was first diagnosed less than a year after her marriage in May of 1992. A year after treatment, she had a happy surprise—Debbie became pregnant with her son, now four years old. When Debbie was diagnosed with breast cancer a second time, in December 1996, her husband told her, "You're getting it fixed and then we're going to go on." Debbie

says her two bouts with cancer have given her "a renewed appreciation of life."

* Zella Harrington is a nineteen-year survivor. She reaches out to newly diagnosed women and shares her motto: "Every day is a good day." In addition to her work as a one-woman support system, Zella enjoys golf, bridge, teaching Sunday school and music. "I don't play piano well enough to please anyone but myself," she says, "but that's good enough for me."

* Gwendolyn Randall was first diagnosed with breast cancer five years ago. A year ago, she experienced a recurrence. Gwendolyn, a volunteer with the Reach to Recovery program, is the third daughter in a family of four children to develop breast cancer. "As difficult as it is, breast cancer is not the end of the world," she says. "Cancer is humbling, but it gave me a new zeal for life—to leave a mark, to be a blessing to people."

* Joan Quicksilver was diagnosed in 1982, "so long ago that sometimes my friends tell me they forget that I ever had it." Joan's initial reaction to the diagnosis was that she was much too busy to die. The day after her surgery, she called in her secretary and got on with the work that was piling up.

* Keryn Shipman, like almost all of the models in the show, found her lump through self-exam. Diagnosed two years ago, she says, "I am walking, living proof that self-exam can save your life. Early detection is the key." Cancer has changed her life. "My attitude is to not let little things stress me anymore," she says. "I appreciate the little things in life, and I have slowed down a lot."

* Diana Holway was diagnosed five years ago. Throughout her treatments and recovery, her family and friends were able to laugh together and cry together, which helped Diana through the hard times. She feels strongly that women should

unite to help fight breast cancer. "It can happen to you," says Diana. "It can happen to you, to your daughter, to the woman sitting next to you."

If it does happen, Diana recommends that you remember to make use of your sense of humor, and, of course, all the models would advocate spending time with your bosom buddies.

April 22, 2000

CHALLENGES OF MID-LIFE

Those of us who once never trusted anyone over thirty had to get over it two decades ago, and now some children of the '60s deny they ever lived by the slogan. Not me. That's who I was then, and as soon as I figure out who I am now, I'll let you know.

I do know it's exciting to be a Baby Boomer, because there always has been strength in numbers. We Baby Boomers have the numbers—there are more of us than of any other generation. Some of us have already turned fifty and received those pesky mailings from the AARP. Some still have that to look forward to. Maybe it's the knowledge that we all are in this together, but we do seem to be a generation that continues to scrutinize conventional wisdom, and sometimes work to alter it, so long after the Summer of Love.

Hey, even if we don't always do something about an issue, at least we talk about everything—including impotence, menopause and death. By doing so, maybe we mid-lifers can continue to make the world a better place for everyone on the planet.

Those Hardening Ovaries

Having conquered the Big O, female Baby Boomers now must turn their attention to the Big M—menopause.

How do I know this?

I know this because women of my acquaintance in their mid-forties suddenly have menopause on their minds. Well, not exactly The Change itself. But Distant Early Warning Signals, such as:

A sudden interest in twenty-two-year-old males with tattoos;

A sudden mood of melancholy;

A sudden frivolity on the part of heretofore reliable monthly cycles;

A sudden preference for calcium-rich foods;

A sudden inexplicable desire to have a baby.

Yep, those all are forerunners of menopause—or so say the latest books on the subject, all written with Baby Boomers in mind.

Gail Sheehy, who counseled us on passages past, gives us *The Silent Passage: Menopause*. Germaine Greer, that feminist firebrand of yore, offers up *The Change: Women, Aging and Menopause*.

Greer quotes Shakespeare, the ancient Greeks, medical textbooks and Emily Dickinson in her book, published by Knopf. She refers to menopause as "the difficult transition from reproductive animal to reflective animal."

She laments that there are women who say they experience nothing significant at this time. Greer chides, "The goal of life is not to feel nothing."

She continues, "The climateric is a time of stock-taking, of spiritual as well as physical change, and it would be a pity to be unconscious of it."

Sheehy's more practical book, from Random House, acknowledges there is little chance of getting through menopause unconsciously, given the Baby Boomers' penchant for the three Rs: Research, Rounding up supporters and Revolution.

Our "generational narcissism," as Sheehy calls it, is hailed by at least one woman in her book. "Perhaps the best gift we can give society," the woman says, "is to see this as something very positive."

In her introduction, Sheehy confides that in spite of her very positive attitude, menopause nearly did her in. Knowledge, she allows, is power, and she titles her first chapter "The Need to Know and the Fear of Knowing."

This sums up what Sheehy thinks about the Change: "Like most graduations, it is the occasion for both relief and sadness."

Frankly, we may need all the help we can get to make it through this particular graduation.

Unsatisfied with resource books found in every conventional bookstore, I dug a little deeper and discovered the Official Goddess Book of Menopause, titled *Wise Woman Ways: Menopausal Years*, by Susun Weed, from Ash Tree Publishing.

Weed is an herbalist, a philosopher, a wise woman for our time, hailed by no less than actress Olympia Dukakis, who contributed a back-cover blurb declaring Weed's work as "vitally important."

That work encompasses alternatives to hormone replacement therapy to a recipe for a dried fruit casserole to flat-out moral support. The foreword, written by a woman named Sher Willis, expresses her thanks to Weed thusly: "Now I understand what menopause is: a time to generate female sexual energy beyond fertility, a season to Change with Earth, and an initiation."

This will not, I predict, be a secret initiation.

Last week, I was having lunch with a friend. We were discussing some worldly matter or other when suddenly she interrupted herself in mid-sentence.

"Wait! Did you hear that? Did you hear that sound?" she said.

I said I hadn't heard anything.

"I think it's my ovaries hardening."

Menopause—here we come!

January 16, 1993

Memory Loss

Feeling dim? Worried that your mental wattage has decreased from 150 to 75?

On some days, maybe even 40?

Relax.

If you're a woman of a certain age, it's probably premenopausal short-term memory loss. (And all this time, I was convinced it was just a full-to-the-brim brain overflowing . . .)

If you're a man—well, I read an article about that somewhere, but I don't remember what it said.

Here's the gist of a phone conversation I had last week:

"Hi. This is Michele. You never got back to me about that brochure on the nature camp in Maine. Do you want to see it?"

"I do! But I called you back the same day I got your message. Remember? I said just put it in the mail or stop by with it next time you're out."

"We didn't talk about this. I'm sure."

"Yeah, we did."

"Maybe we did. Did we?"

"I'm not sure, but I think so."

And so it goes. We laughed about it because neither of us was certain.

Michele did remember to mail it, and I read it. It was great! It's around here somewhere. . . .

Michele said she has goofy conversations every day with a friend she walks with. Half the time, she said, they can't remember what they are telling one another or even how to tell it.

"What's weird is that we understand each other anyway," she said.

I remember all this because I wrote it down.

In *The Silent Passage*, her book on menopause, Gail Sheehy refers to this short-term memory loss as "a little fuzzy thinking in the early years of the Change of Life."

"The temporary strain on short-term memory is quantifiable, but women are not seriously impaired in their daily functioning," Sheehy writes.

Lonnie Barbach also has written a book on menopause. In *The Pause*, she writes: "Some women going through The Pause complain about a loss of mental acuity, problems with short-term memory loss and an inability to concentrate."

Both authors refer to studies by Dr. Bruce McEwen, a neuro-endocrinologist at Rockefeller University. Good news! He says "the subjective experience of cloudy thinking at times during menopause can be equated to jet lag. It's mostly transient and certainly reversible."

Blame it on hormone fluctuation. The same thing happens when you're pregnant. Remember?

Not every woman experiences short-term memory loss during early menopause, Barbach says. Those who do, Barbach writes, "devise fail-safe techniques to augment their capricious memories."

Some of us write everything down. Some of us start counting on our kids or spouses to do for us what we've done for them for years. And some of us assign a place for everything and we keep everything in its place or we'd never find it again.

Some of us learn to laugh about it.

Here's what I wrote at the end of a letter to a friend in California: "I can't remember what I say to anybody anymore. If I've already written to you about all the above, please forgive me and pass this letter on to someone I haven't told."

I do remember that I've written before about the wily symptoms of early menopause. It was just after a friend of mine announced in a restaurant that she thought she could hear her ovaries hardening over lunch.

In that column, I enumerated four specific symptoms. A reader called a day or two later to ask why I had not mentioned short-term memory loss.

I told her the truth.

I forgot.

October 9, 1993

Old Eggs

Old Eggs, they tell us, often are responsible for mental retardation or chromosomal abnormalities in babies born to middle-aged women.

Old Eggs, we middle-aged women tell one another, are

the origin of these absolutely ridiculous inclinations to have one last baby.

The Old Eggs talk directly to us; they whisper and mutter among themselves and then shout in unison: "Have another baby before it's too late!"

"I find myself thinking way too much about babies," says one friend, forty-six. She works full-time and plans to begin a doctoral program next year. But her Old Eggs are talking, and sometimes she is overwhelmed by the need to care for a baby one last time.

She adds that her two teen-agers would be embarrassed if she did. Also, her husband is not too keen on the idea.

"No," he said, not unkindly, when she confessed her yearnings. "No, we can't do that."

Actually, we can—for a little while longer, anyway.

Whether we really want to or we're simply under the spell of those meddling Old Eggs is another question altogether.

Certainly, we have other matters on our minds. To wit: Paying college tuition, fretting over the incidence of breast cancer among women our age, mapping out a starvation diet so we can get down to 119 pounds (the weight a new study deems appropriate for every middle-aged woman on Earth), pondering the possibilities for progress in the wake of the U.N. World Conference on Women.

We're busy! But I digress.

My friend said she has come full circle.

Time was, in her early days of mothering, she was delighted to be in the presence of wee ones. As her children grew, her tolerance for shrieking infants lessened. Eventually, the high-pitched screams of children put her severely on edge.

"I've changed again," she said. "Something's different. Now I'm drawn to children again."

My friends and I had babies back when new mothers did not go to the mall the day after the baby was born. We didn't go the next week, either. We stayed in, nesting with the new one, for a month or more. We were fortunate in that none of us had to return to work right away.

We were, I guess, Earth Mothers.

"I used to sneer at Earth Mothers," my friend said. "I know I was one, once, but over the years I became quite disdainful of women I would see interacting with their children in that all-encompassing, Earth Mother sort of way.

"Now I want to be one again."

One friend, a little older than the rest of us, said she remembers a few scattered messages from her Old Eggs, but she ignored them and passed through that phase.

Another friend said her time is taken up by her family in its current incarnation, and she won't be looking at layettes anytime soon. I hear from my Old Eggs from time to time, but I hush them, telling them to stop being so impractical.

There is, of course, another solution.

"Have a baby," I said to my friend. "We'll all help take care of it!"

She laughed.

Then she recited part of a poem that makes her cry. Sharon Olds, an award-winning poet, wrote it. In the poem, Olds writes of watching her daughter come of age:

as my last chances to bear a child
are falling through my body, the duds among them,
her full purse of eggs, round and
firm as hard-boiled yolks, is about
to snap its clasp.

Olds, we middle-aged women tell ourselves, understands about Old Eggs. Still, we hear ours talking. Do you hear yours?

September 30, 1995

Cleaning Out the Closet

The purchase of one grown-up-lady dress recently has prompted an identity crisis in my house. I'd like to tell you that the person having the crisis is my teen-age daughter, but I don't have one. It's me.

When I brought the dress home, I realized I needed to clean out my closets. I have two, which is more than a person needs but not as many closets as some people have. The new dress prompted an urgent need in me to weed out clothes I no longer like or wear. Out with the old, and in with the new, as it were.

The problem with that is that I'm no longer the me who chose those old clothes, but I'm not necessarily a new me with a defined taste in new clothes, either—or the money to start all over. I called a friend to ask just who I am right now.

"I have no idea," she said. "I do know I've decided to take thirty or so of my little wool dresses to the resell-it shop. I'm not somebody who wears little wool dresses anymore."

She also has all but given up pantyhose, and she used to like them so well that I swear she slept in them. This same friend once returned a pair of white shoes to a department store, explaining to the clerk that they were "too white" for her at that point in her personal evolution.

To be fair, she's been shoe shopping with me when I've rejected numerous pairs for having heels that are too high or too low, toes that are too round or too pointy and styles that are too fussy or too plain. We both know what we like when we see it—and usually, it's a pair of shoes that looks just like two or three pairs we already own.

This same friend just bought a blazer and a jacket, neither

of which she suspects she will ever wear. The sale was too good to pass up, she said.

Besides, the blazer and the jacket fit her right this minute. After she lost about forty pounds, she gave away her large clothes. When she gained some of the weight back, she gave away some of her small clothes. She said she doesn't have a lot of medium clothes, so even though the new blazer and jacket don't quite suit her image of herself right now, at least they are the right size.

Her advice to me the other evening was this: "You might go back to being someone like the person you used to be, so I don't think I'd get rid of anything now just because you're in transition to someone new. But maybe you would feel better if you got rid of a trash bag full of shoes. It always works for me."

Neither of us really has *that* many shoes, but I knew what she meant, and headed for the closet. What we both do have is a passion for shoes, which also is the name of a fabulous book by Linda Sunshine and Mary Tiegreen. Andrews and McMeel published the book, advertised as "The perfect book for anyone with two feet and $10.95."

A Passion for Shoes includes thoughts on shoes by such diverse writers as Oscar Wilde, Dorothy Parker, Woody Allen, Diana Vreeland and Gilda Radner. Color illustrations include archival photos from shoe designers, cartoons, photographs, advertisements—we're talking lots of pictures of shoes of all sorts, and rumba instructions to boot. (Sorry.)

I called another friend and explained that I was eager to clean out closets but wasn't sure what to keep and what to get rid of.

"I'm the worst person to ask," she said. "I have way too many clothes." She explained that she buys clothes for who she is now, who she once was and who she might be later on. It works for her because she has room to store the clothes until she grows into them psychologically.

"When I bought that wearable art jacket all those years ago, I knew I would wear it someday, just not then. I'm starting to wear it now," she said. She does feel guilty, as we all do, about owning clothing that is not being put to good use, but she has trouble turning loose of most of it.

Next, I called a male friend.

"What's the big deal? Get rid of anything you haven't worn in six months," he said. "People only wear the same four things over and over anyway, and there is no point in having stuff you don't wear."

I explained that some of the stuff I don't wear is really pretty and looks nice on me, too.

"Then why don't you wear it?" he asked.

"Because I don't have the right shoes," I said.

"No man has ever had that problem," he said. "Just get rid of it." Then he made some excuse to hang up. Clearly, he knows who he is—and what to wear.

Tell me I'm not the only one—do you waste time worrying about what's in your wardrobe, what isn't and what to do about it?

October 5, 1996

Eighteen, Now and Forever

When I graduated from high school thirty-one years ago, no one told me what I most needed to know. As a favor to seniors everywhere, I've decided to speak up so you don't waste time not knowing now what I wish I had known then.

Here it is: In terms of values and tastes and habits, you

probably are at eighteen much the same person you will be at forty-eight. That's not to say that life won't bring you rich and varied experiences that may change how you perceive the world or yourself, but your essence, your core self, likely is in place right this minute.

The decision to reveal this secret was based not on whim, but on solid research. In the past few weeks, I've randomly asked people of various ages if they think they are the same people they were at eighteen. Every one of them said no. Then, as they began to speak of their likes and dislikes, basic beliefs, habits good and bad and other characteristics, they conceded that some essential self, in place at eighteen, was still minding the store.

Here's how it works: If you're basically happy, you'll stay basically happy. If you whine now, you'll probably be whining thirty years hence. If you're overly organized and show up ten minutes early for everything, that probably won't change. If you're more laid back and get there when you get there, that's a pattern you may stick with.

If you're crazy about suede Mary Jane shoes and spend most of your money on music and books, expect to have a house thirty years from now full of shoes, music and books. If you feel guilty about spending money on yourself now, you'll likely still be hard on yourself in years to come.

If jeans and a T-shirt are your ensemble of choice now, you won't give that up. If lying in bed with your dog, a bag of Doritos and a good book strikes you as a perfect way to spend an afternoon now, why would you think that's a passing fancy? Say you routinely order a double cheeseburger with ketchup and extra pickles every time you go to Steak 'n' Shake. Even after you can afford to order rare beef tenderloin at the finest of restaurants, you will sometimes find yourself at the drive-through window, picking up that very burger.

I'm not saying you will never change. Life has a way of issuing challenges, teaching lessons, altering perceptions that will cause you to think or act differently than you do now. Learning is what life is all about, and you will have plenty of experiences, make many mistakes, try many new things, that will help you learn.

I knew that when I was eighteen. Where I went wrong was that I thought that every pore of my being was subject to change. For instance, my friend Susan and I were under the impression that if we just waited long enough, true happiness would come to us.

"Won't it be wonderful when we're happy?" we'd say. We wasted a lot of time by not taking responsibility for our own happiness.

Also, we were influenced by "Father Knows Best," "Leave It to Beaver" and other cloying sitcoms of the time. Under the spell of all those TV moms in angora sweaters and pearls, I thought for a long time that my red and purple paisley soul gradually would fade to gentle, muted tones and that I'd take up vacuuming in heels, even though my own mother never did anything of the kind. It never happened, and I remember actually being disappointed—for a while.

Today, eighteen-year-olds appear far more confident than most members of my generation, but just in case the self-esteem is an act, know that the sooner you decide to like yourself and to cultivate your most admirable characteristics, the better. Once you've declared yourself worthy of whatever you seek in life, you can get on with seeking it and stop fretting over your imperfections.

I'm not saying that you can't work at being more muscular, far kinder, more prompt, less antsy or even musically inclined. Just know that everyone faces personal challenges, and, once acknowledged, they simply do not need to occupy your every waking thought.

The late Diana Vreeland, a hero of mine, knew what she was talking about when she said that you dare not spend your life looking behind you to see who is about to catch up. You have to keep your eye on your goal, and fulfill it as only as you can, no matter who is bringing up the rear.

OK, let's review: You are who you are, and chances are good that you will remain true to yourself at twenty-eight, thirty-eight and forty-eight—and probably beyond. Thirty years from now, you will look different, but inside, you'll have lots of qualities that date back to the day you graduated from high school.

My advice now that you're graduating from high school— and thanks for asking—is this: Live with great purpose every day, just in case you don't get as many days on the planet as you'd hoped. Love yourself and others. Laugh a lot. Do work that matters to you. Choose peace over conflict, and take responsibility for your own happiness.

After all, you're only eighteen once. Chronologically, anyway.

June 7, 1997

Moving Choices

When you move, you have to touch everything you own. With each item, you have to ask yourself whether you want to keep it, give it away or toss it in the trash. This process involves some laughter and some tears as you encounter the strange and wonderful, which so often is packed away in the basement.

One recent evening, my son and I cleaned out a small

room in the basement with a large storage closet. As we sat and sorted, Joel, twenty-three, confronted his natural resistance to change. Even at age five, he cried for days when we traded in an old car for a new one. Joel has a flair for the dramatic that I may be responsible for genetically, so I tried not to buy into his more outrageous statements.

"I don't like this," Joel said at one point. "You are asking me to remove all evidence of myself from your life."

I replied that in truth, I was simply asking him to box up some of his childhood books and toys and store them at his dad's, as my new condo has less storage than my current home. "Well, OK," he said. "But you definitely are asking me to say good-bye to my childhood home."

That's not so, I countered. I reminded him that his childhood home was elsewhere in Shrewsbury and that we moved from that house when he was six.

Ever eager to make his point, Joel then declared that surely I was upset about leaving my childhood home. "Actually, this isn't my childhood home, either. I grew up in the city, and my family moved here when I was twelve. You know that," I said.

"Still . . ." he started, and then let it drop.

Joel sat sorting through stuffed animals from his childhood, clearly upset about asking them to leave their childhood home. "I don't really want Grover anymore, and if I pack him in a box, I know I'll never look at him again," Joel said. "But I don't want to throw him away, either."

I told him that almost everybody in this country has a box full of old stuffed animals, loved long ago and now all but forgotten. To prove it, I showed him the stuffed dog I got when I was four while seeing Santa Claus at a department store.

"Dad has a big basement, so keep a few favorites and let the rest go," I said.

Then it was my turn to struggle. I opened a box, packed by my late mother, full of my little brother's things—assorted handmade wooden boats, a pencil holder made in Cub Scouts and a collection of baseball caps. Michael died in 1963 of kidney disease, a few days shy of his tenth birthday and a month before my fifteenth. I took out three of the items from the box and set them aside, and I put the rest in the trash.

"How can you do that?" Joel asked.

"I have to do that," I said. "This box has been sitting on a shelf for thirty-five years. My mother doesn't need these things. Michael doesn't need these things. I need to keep just a few of them, honor the rest for a minute and then let them go."

Emboldened by my brave words, I next threw out every essay I had written in junior high school, black-and-white photos taken on the senior trip to Washington, D.C., and a stack of notes from my best friend Susan that all read, "I'll be home from camp about 7:30 p.m. on Friday."

As I continued to fill trash bags, I pointed out to Joel that I was saving him a lot of work. "When you move, you have to touch everything you own," I said. "Someone else has to touch it all when you die. Because I'm throwing away so much stuff now, you won't have much to do when the day comes that you have to go through my things."

Was he grateful? I'm not sure.

As we worked side by side, I entertained him with funny stories about getting ready to move. My favorite is about the day I walked into a hardware store. A young clerk immediately asked what he might help me find.

"Switch plates," I said.

He led me to a selection of utility knives, thinking I was in the market for a switchblade.

In addition to switch plates for the new place, I also

bought a real bed. I'm a big fan of free-flow waterbeds, but I'm not so fond of waterbed furniture, which all looks very '70s. I wanted new furniture, so I compromised and bought a soft-side waterbed, a regular mattress with a bag of water and thermostat tucked inside, so you don't have to give up any of the benefits of sleeping on a waterbed. Soft-side mattresses may be used with conventional furniture and conventional sheets, so you can kiss the '70s furniture and the custom-made linens good-bye. I had meant to buy a sleigh bed, but a different sort of bed took my breath away, and now it's on order.

"I'm growing up," I told friends. "I bought a grown-up bed." They asked what kind. "A four-poster, fit for a fairy princess."

September 19, 1998

Make Noise Now!

So I'm attending Diversity Training, and we're watching a video. We see store clerks racing to assist a white man but ignoring a black customer. I whisper to a woman sitting near me that most store clerks don't want to wait on anyone. "Well," she says, "they certainly don't want to wait on women our age."

She's right. Women over fifty find themselves at the earliest stages of becoming invisible. Never mind that we still dress young, think young, feel young. Alas, we are beginning to look old, and to younger store clerks, "old" often translates as "boring," unworthy of respect or time.

Here we are, coping with empty-nest syndrome, adjusting our under-funded retirement plans and wondering whether it's too late to be a baseball umpire instead, and we're being tuned out by part of the population. Then there are the physical changes. Nuala O'Faolain nails this aspect in her poignant book *Are You Somebody?* (Owl Books, $11.95):

"I note every day the physical detail of middle age. The transparent polyps that have formed on the skin of my neck. The first white hair in my eyebrows. Pigment spots on my midriff, which will never tan again. . . . . How do people arrange to love their aging selves?"

The crone movement, a call for conscious aging as women enter the last trimester of their lives, helps bring peace of mind. Margaret Mead tipped us off about "post-menopausal zest." Even Colette sounded positive when she wrote in her seventies: "Love, one of the great commonplaces of existence, is slowly leaving mine. The maternal instinct is another great commonplace. Once we've left these behind, we find that all the rest is gay and varied."

Just try trading on inner self-confidence when you're in a store. I thought about this just last week, when I added two more places to my list of "Stores I Won't Go To Anymore."

Here is what happened: First, I stopped in a copy place. I stood alone at an empty counter for a full five minutes. When a young woman finally appeared, I said I wanted to print out digital photos on photo-quality paper. She said I was at the wrong counter. At the right counter, a young man told me I could leave my disc for a couple of hours or I could print the photos myself for much less money. I said I was game. He spent fifteen seconds with me, rattling off the steps I needed to take to print the pictures.

I keyed in the commands and returned to the first counter, where I said I was waiting for my pictures on photo-quality paper. "Oh," said a young woman, "our machine is jamming. This could take hours. You'd better just leave everything here."

Just about then, one of my pictures popped out of the printer. It was on flimsy paper. I said for the third time that I wanted the pictures on photo-quality paper. The young woman said they didn't dare put heavier stock into the printer, as it was already jamming. A young man who arrived to take apart the printer advised me to leave my disc as I likely wouldn't get any photos right away.

"One already printed," I said, waving it at him. "It's fine, but I want it on photo-quality paper."

"We don't do that," he said.

Twenty minutes I'm in this store, and now I find out they don't have what I came in to get, even though I've been talking about it since I arrived. While this little shock registered, my other photos slid out of the printer.

"Give them to me," I said. "Never mind that this is not what I wanted. This is what I got." The good news? The clerk at the first counter had no idea what price the clerk at the second counter had quoted me, and I was charged about half. That's fair, I thought, and I left. I won't be back.

Later in the day, I went into a store that wants you to organize your life in their plastic bins, which come in all sizes, colors and shapes. I needed picture frames and wrapping paper. I found them and got in the shorter of the two check-out lines. I was behind a family of three that was returning an item and re-buying it for a discounted price. It took forever, or at least ten minutes. Finally—my turn! Then I heard the clerk say, "I'll help you take this to your car." And off he went, "helping" with the same merchandise that the family had carried into the store.

I spread my merchandise all over the counter. Then, in a voice that I managed to project all the way to the clerk's retreating back, I said, "You might have mentioned that you had no intention of waiting on me."

I left, and I won't be back. Hey, maybe we're becoming invisible, but we still can be, and must be, heard.

June 26, 1999

Chapter 8

FAVORITE ANIMAL FRIENDS

Some of my best friends are elephants. No, really. I love animals. I've admired African elephants in Tanzania, and I've felt that same sense of privilege while visiting the Asian elephants at the St. Louis Zoo. Someday, I want to run away from home and work with elephants at Amboseli National Park in Kenya.

If it were legal, I'd have my own rhino, or maybe a hippo or even a takin. I grew up with dogs and birds, and I now live with cats. And since 1982, I've traveled all over the world to see whales in their natural habitat. A female teen-age gray whale in San Ignacio Lagoon once wrapped her mouth around my right arm—but I digress.

This book just wouldn't be complete without a nod to some of my friends in the animal world.

Pregnant Pearl

Pearl is pregnant for the first time. So far, everything is going well.

She is twenty, a single mother who lives with four friends. The father lives in Springfield, Missouri, and probably won't be involved in the birth or the rearing of the infant.

Pearl is gaining weight, of course—six to seven pounds a day for the last month. Whoa, you're thinking. That's almost fifty pounds a week—what kind of elephant is this Pearl?

Asian, actually. Pearl lives at the St. Louis Zoo with four other elephants—Clara, Marie, Carolyn and Donna.

Last week, I dropped by the Zoo to talk babies. I was greeted with some enthusiastic trunk nuzzling and a great deal of information about pregnant elephants. It was Pearl who did the nuzzling, and my sweatshirt bore visual and aromatic traces of same for the rest of the day.

The information came primarily from Tim O'Sullivan, head keeper at the Elephant House.

O'Sullivan said that Pearl eats up to ten pounds of vegetables, twenty-nine pounds of grain and sixty pounds of hay every day. And because she's eating for two, Pearl sometimes protects her share of the food by smacking young Donna.

Hey, every pregnant female has her moods.

Pearl has been pregnant for ten months, and she won't deliver until late this year or early next. Being pregnant for twenty-two months would make anyone moody. If her pregnancy comes to term, Pearl will deliver the first elephant ever born at the Zoo.

That's exciting for Zoo visitors, but elephant lovers everywhere also will rejoice, because right now there is a shortage of Asian elephants in the world. Fewer than 35,000 are left in the wild. Their habitat has been destroyed, and the animals have been slaughtered for their ivory tusks. Only seventy-five calves have been born in captivity. If we lose Asian elephants, we can't make more. Extinct is forever.

In the wild, a pregnant elephant ready to deliver moves off from the herd, and usually a female companion, called an "auntie," accompanies her to watch for predators that may try to strike during the birth.

When her labor commences, Pearl will be isolated from the other elephants for her protection. Just a few people will be present for the birth, but like many modern mothers, Pearl will have her delivery videotaped.

Because baby elephants are rambunctious—they tumble and climb and run around—the Zoo is baby-proofing the elephant yard, building barriers along the moats to protect the baby from falling in or from being accidentally bumped in by one of the adult elephants.

The father-to-be is twenty-seven-year-old Onyx, an Asian bull elephant who weighs in at about 10,000 pounds. Onyx lives at the Dickerson Park Zoo in Springfield. Pearl and Carolyn visited Springfield for six months last year specifically to get to know Onyx. Apparently, Pearl and Onyx got to know each other very well.

Usually a trim 5,328 pounds, Pearl has gained 600 to 800 pounds since her pregnancy began. She's up to 6,233 pounds. At birth, the baby will weigh 150 to 300 pounds.

Hormonal changes have caused Pearl to grow what is politely referred to as superfluous body hair, and her mammary glands are developing, gearing up to feed an infant.

Are her feet swollen? Does she suffer from terminal indigestion? Does she crave beef-and-bean burritos in the middle of the night, or perhaps lust after fresh California plums in January?

No, says O'Sullivan, one of a veritable herd of surrogate fathers-to-be at the Zoo.

Basically, Pearl is still the sweet, slightly nervous elephant she always has been.

Except now she's pregnant.

January 25, 1992

Elephant Midwife Watch

Pearl, the pregnant elephant at the St. Louis Zoo, greeted me early this week with her tail sticking straight out and her left hind leg raised off the floor.

Those are signs of labor in elephants. I know that because last month I attended a two-hour training session and watched videos of elephants in labor. I'm a member of the elephant "midwife watch" team, volunteers who take turns keeping an eye on Pearl now that her time is near.

When we check in at the Elephant House, we turn on a closed-circuit monitor so we can watch Pearl, who is just across the hall. There she was, holding up a hind leg and sticking her tail straight out.

We volunteers were told it was unlikely that we would see any signs of labor. The Zoo staff anticipated that a blood test, administered daily, would tip them off when Pearl was about to go into labor, and at that point, the staff would start a twenty-four-hour watch.

Yet there I was, looking at obvious signs of labor in a 7,100-pound elephant expecting a 200-pound calf—the Zoo's first baby elephant. I called Bill Houston, associate curator at the Zoo.

"Bill! She's got her tail stuck out and she's lifting her hind legs!" I said, my heart pounding.

"Watch her for ten or fifteen more minutes and call me back," he said.

I stared at the monitor. Throaty rumbles echoed through the building. They might have come from Pearl or it might have been me.

Bill and I talked again. He asked me to quickly scan five hours of tape recorded earlier to see when Pearl first started behaving oddly. I watched intently, eyes glued to the screen and ears tuned in to catch the slightest sound from Pearl and the four elephants with whom she shares a stall.

Suddenly I heard what I thought was a large animal exhaling hard. I was certain it was not me.

I switched off the tape to watch the elephants on "real time." Pearl was leaning against the wall, inhaling and exhaling deeply. Her entire body rippled with the effort.

"I'm trying to be objective," I gasped breathlessly to Bill on the phone, "but I think she's pushing."

He said she might be snoring. He might be right. My experience watching elephants in labor—or sleeping, for that matter—is limited. However, I have given birth.

My lower back started to hurt. I shifted in my chair, trying to get comfortable. I went back to the tape. There was Pearl, lying down and then getting up three times in quick succession. That's another sign of labor.

I went over to the locked door that leads to the public area and peeked through a crack at Pearl. She looked right at me. She stuck out her tail and raised her right hind leg.

"I'm calling Bill right now to ask him to come," I said softly.

While I waited for Bill, I thought about Elly, the cat that lived in the Elephant House for twenty-one years. She chased mice, visited with the rhinos and often slept cuddled next to an elderly tapir named Grandpa. She died last week. A sudden death, I thought, and soon, a birth.

Bill and I watched Pearl into the wee hours of the morning until she settled down and went to sleep.

The next day, Bill told me that the elephant keepers believe what we saw was either the baby moving around— maybe into position in the birth canal—or the elephant equivalent of Braxton-Hicks contractions, which are warm-up sessions for the uterus, getting ready for the big job ahead.

Driving home that morning after I left the Elephant House, I remembered that Pearl is an Asian elephant. As such, she may come under the care of Ganesha, the elephant-headed Hindi god that specializes in removing all obstacles and represents good fortune for all beginnings.

I sent a little prayer off to Ganesha on Pearl's behalf.

December 12, 1992

Elephant Power Play

Maybe you've heard about the Elephant Wars at the St. Louis Zoo. Maybe you've even witnessed a skirmish or two and wondered what's up.

Apparently, Donna, the lowest elephant in the herd's hierarchy, is making a play to increase her standing. She's been fighting with Clara, the matriarch, and both animals have sustained some injuries.

For those of you not intimately acquainted with the local elephant population, here's who's who: The Zoo houses five female elephants: Clara, forty years old; Marie, also forty; Carolyn, twenty-six; Pearl, twenty-one; and Donna, also twenty-one. Raja, Pearl's calf, is the only male. He was born December 27 and now weighs about 570 pounds, more than twice his birth weight of 275.

Tim O'Sullivan, head elephant keeper, says that traditionally, all the adult elephants have respected Clara's position as head of the herd. But in the past six weeks, Donna has gone head to head—literally—with Clara several times. When elephants fight, they butt heads.

"This is all normal behavior," O'Sullivan said. "This happens in the wild, too. Elephants about Donna's age start flexing their muscle. It's our policy not to interrupt fights. We let the elephants be elephants."

Clara and Donna are about the same height and each weighs about 6,700 pounds, O'Sullivan said. But Clara has twenty years on Donna and the experience that only years can bring. About twenty years ago, Clara took the title of matriarch from an elephant named Trudy. Some say Clara ascended before Trudy's death; others say afterward, but everyone remembers fights between Clara and Trudy.

On March 9, Donna picked a fight with Clara. The two butted heads for about fifteen minutes, and then Donna moved away. With her trunk, Clara smacked Donna on the belly a few times to reinforce her dominance. For the rest of the day, Donna exhibited submissive behaviors, such as backing up to Clara.

The next morning, keepers discovered about six inches of Donna's tail had been bitten off. They suspect either Donna issued another challenge or Clara simply wanted to make it very clear that she was in charge. Donna was moved to a private stall for a few days to heal. When she was reunited with the others, she appeared to have resumed her usual place in the herd, O'Sullivan said.

Donna once enjoyed a higher position in the herd. When the Zoo sent Pearl and Carolyn to the Dickerson Park Zoo in Springfield, Missouri, to mate with Onyx, Donna stayed behind.

"She was still last, behind Marie and Clara, but there were two fewer elephants here, and that may have boosted her confidence," O'Sullivan said. "When Pearl and Carolyn came back, Donna had to move back down the ladder. Then Pearl, who had been Donna's playmate, gave birth to Raja, and that changed Pearl's behavior toward Donna. That could be part of the problem too."

O'Sullivan added that Raja's exuberant presence "has added stress to the social structure." He walks all over the other elephants' food, he literally runs into them as he careens around the stall in search of new adventures and, in general, disrupts the harmony of the herd.

Early in April, Donna started pestering Clara again. A videotape made on April 3 showed Donna and Clara fussing all night long, though they were in separate stalls.

"They were fighting through the gate, butting their heads on the bars between them, and they both had some superficial wounds the next morning," O'Sullivan said. "On Sunday, fifteen minutes after we put them in the same stall, Donna was in Clara's face."

O'Sullivan said that for about ninety minutes, there was a lot of pushing and shoving, grabbing of trunks, ear biting and tail biting.

"At one point, Clara butted heads with Donna, and Donna tripped on a ledge in the stall," he said. "She fell on her left side, which is weaker than her right side. Donna couldn't get up, and Clara kept smacking her."

The keepers intervened. They moved the other elephants

from the stall and helped Donna back on her feet. Since then, Donna has been separated from the herd.

"We need to get Donna outside and let her blow off steam," O'Sullivan said, noting that some yard work remains to be done before all six elephants may go outdoors. "Some of the problem could be due to cabin fever. When they are outside, they all have more room. Still, I don't think this particular battle is over."

Stay tuned—it's all happening at the Zoo.
April 17, 1993

Vultures in Africa

So we're tooling along a dirt road on the floor of Ngorongoro Crater in Tanzania, and we come upon a kill.

That's a dead animal, brought down by another animal.

I had suspected I might run into just such a situation during a two-week safari, but I wasn't sure how I would react if I had to confront a dead animal in person. A friend at the office has tried over the years to teach me that there are no senior citizens' residences in the wild. There are no neonatal units for baby animals born with defects, no walk-in clinics, no hospices. No Band-Aids and Neosporin, even.

Only animals in perfect health live in Africa.

(Those animals die, too, if some rich man decides he wants a buffalo head on his living room wall or an umbrella stand made from an elephant's leg or some ground rhino horn to make him think he is sexy. But that's another story.)

Predators kill the weak, the old, the sick and the malformed. That's nature, and it's not pretty. Hyenas attend wildebeest births. If the baby isn't strong enough to be up on its feet in three minutes and able to run twenty minutes after it pops out, the mother wildebeest is soon calfless.

I've seen predators and prey on television. Ngorongoro Crater isn't television.

Lying close to the road was a wildebeest, or what was left of it—a head and a few ribs. The lion or hyena that had killed the animal had eaten or hauled off the rest.

When we drove up, the carcass was covered by vultures. My more educated traveling companions knew exactly which vultures and other birds of prey were fighting over the tasty bits of dead wildebeest.

I knew only that I'd never seen anything so remarkable.

The birds hissed, squawked and clawed at one another, fighting for the best position. One gripped another's head in its talons, and the stronger bird shoved its victim down under the carcass.

Then the 747 of vultures came in for a landing. When the birds already there complained, the forty-inch-tall black bird puffed out its chest, draped its broad wings around itself and stalked toward the smaller birds. The big guy, who looked like Frank Langella in *Dracula*, said nothing.

I spoke up.

"That's a turkey vulture," I whispered to the woman next to me in the van. "I know one—his name is Hoover, and he lives at the World Bird Sanctuary in St. Louis County."

Our driver whispered that the bird in question was a Nubian vulture, also known as a lappet-faced vulture. They are Old World vultures, and not at all related to the turkey vulture, which is a New World vulture.

A Nubian vulture! I once made the acquaintance of a splendid Nubian goat named How About Them Apples, and I was delighted to meet his countryman.

I stood up again (we were in roofless Land Rovers) to observe the carnage through my binoculars. Then I squealed, which is considered bad behavior on a game drive. You're supposed to be quiet, so you don't disturb the animals.

I squealed because I remembered that some people regard the working press as vultures.

Not those who truly know and love us, of course, and not those who have benefited directly from the sensitivity most of us show to strangers suffering personal tragedy. But there are people—usually politicians trying to get away with something—who have made references to the press "picking the carcass clean" before flying off to the next feeding.

I lost my heart to journalism thirty years ago, and I'm proud of what I do. So even though I was quite taken with the Nubian vulture, and I learned a lot about life and death on the African plains by watching the big birds play their part, I didn't identify with it.

I did come to feel close to another African bird, one with less offensive personal habits. I speak of a ground-dwelling bird, described in my field guide as "long-necked and long-legged, with a robust body and short bill." These birds are known for their spectacular courtship displays.

I especially like this particular bird for its name, and have decided to petition the court immediately to change my name to Kori Bustard.

Look out, Wolf Blitzer!

August 7, 1993

A Spider on the Porch

A spider set up housekeeping at my place last week. Never before have I stood around on my front porch talking to a spider, and never again will I pass up that opportunity.

Here's the deal: I speak to strange cats and dogs, I wave and call out to cows and other farm animals in fields. I acknowledge the presence of every bird I see. At the Zoo, I whisper in Swahili to the African animals and in English to the others.

Some people think I'm crazy. I consider my life enriched because I take time to appreciate species other than my own.

Yet when it comes to spiders, I am not particularly informed. I once interviewed a man while a pink-toed tarantula walked up and down his arm, but generally I live and let live when it comes to eight-legged beasties.

This particular spider spun a web on my front porch, between the railing and the awning. The web was big—maybe four feet by three feet—and of a complex design. I first saw it when I came home Sunday evening. The porch light fully illuminated the web, which had not been there earlier in the day. Astonished, I stopped and traced the intricate design with my eyes.

At the top of the web crouched a spider.

"You've been busy," I said aloud. "Good hunting!" Then I went inside and thought no more about it.

The next morning when I popped out the door to get the newspaper, the spider was in a corner of the web, futzing with a dead moth. In the sunlight, I could see her reddish-orange coloration better. I was surprised to see that her body was about the size of a dime.

I went inside to find some sort of reference book to learn

about what I was looking at. I found only one book in the house on spiders—E.B. White's *Charlotte's Web*.

Charlotte, of course, was a gray spider who conspired with a rat to save a pig's life. She was a well-spoken spider, and always greeted Wilbur (that's the pig) by saying, "Salutations."

Well, what would you have done?

I opened the door, leaned out and said, "Salutations."

Then I called George Winkler, the chief entomologist at the St. Louis Zoo. I described the spider and the web to him, and he said an orb weaver had found her way to my front porch. He also said the spider's days were numbered.

"Orb weavers are programmed to die in the fall," he said. "She may lay an egg case, and she may not, and it may or may not be fertilized. But she won't last much longer."

From the Powder Valley Conservation Nature Center in Kirkwood, I got a booklet on spiders. I learned that more than 300 species live in Missouri and that spiders have been on Earth for 400 million years.

Why did I wait so long to notice?

Before I left for work the next day, I stood for a long time on the porch, staring at the spider and her web.

This, I think, is what life is all about—learning about our surroundings and understanding where we fit in.

Four days after I first saw the orb weaver, I came home to find her web torn at one edge of the railing. The next day, all that was left was the single strand she had used to swing from the roof to the awning.

I miss her.

A few years ago, a friend who was depressed said she couldn't think of a single reason to go on. I blurted out that I still want to learn about seashells, cacti and wildflowers.

Add spiders to that list.

October 16, 1993

Ginger and Scoop and Maggie

I invited someone new into my bed. An adjustment period is always required in these matters. At first, I woke up every time he leapt out of bed to go to the kitchen for a snack or to check out a noise in the living room.

Now, I hardly notice.

I'm even learning to sleep through it when he cuddles close, begins to purr and drools all over me.

The "he" I speak of is Ginger, my ten-year-old orange cat. For much of his life, we slept separately.

I am very serious about my sleeping, so I always slept alone and the two cats, Scoop and Ginger, slept together. But on Thanksgiving, when we first learned that Scoop had diseased lungs, I opened my bedroom door and welcomed them both into my bed.

They slept quite comfortably, right away.

Me, I sat bolt upright every time either of them jumped off the bed. Where are they going? What are they doing? Is Scoop in trouble? Is Ginger OK? Oops! Do I hear someone throwing up in the den?

Well, you get the picture.

I also had to forgo my favorite sleeping position, the diagonal enchilada, where I roll around until I've tucked the covers under me on both sides and then stretch out diagonally. I tried to sleep on just one side of the bed, but the cats moved around a lot in the night, and I constantly worried about kicking them. Also, I didn't want to accidentally bounce either of them out of my queen-size waterbed.

And so it went.

Then the day came that Scoop's breathing was more labored than ever, and he took to hiding in the back of my closet. I realized I had to find the courage to stop trying this medical intervention or putting hope in that treatment, to stop hassling my furry orange friend who clearly was close to the end of his life.

"It's peaceful," my friend Philip had said of euthanasia. "You think it's going to be scary and horrible, but it's not. It's very quiet, and very peaceful."

I thought about that a lot. I carried Scoop around the house for a while, crying on his furry little head. I called my son, who is away at college, for moral support. Then I took Scoop to the veterinarian, where I petted him and whispered to him as he died.

It was peaceful. It was quiet. And it was the right thing to do.

I came home and tried to hold Ginger, but he was more interested in napping. That night when I went to bed, Ginger joined me once again, and I was glad to have the company.

At this point, I am fairly accustomed to his nocturnal meanderings. I no longer hop up, worried and scared that something is wrong. In fact, I enjoy having him share my bed, even when he stomps across my abdomen at 3 a.m., meowing about something he thinks is important. Somehow, I feel like Colette.

Now it's Ginger's turn to hop up, worried and scared.

A month ago, I adopted a two-year-old brown tortoise shell cat named Maggie through the Cat Network, a rescue service.

Maggie had been rescued off the streets about a year ago and then had lived happily in a foster home with other cats and dogs for another year. Her foster mother hoped to find a quieter home for Maggie, who is very shy.

When I first saw her, she was in a wire cage at the Petsmart store in Sunset Hills, lying in her litter pan and covering her eyes with one paw. It was her first time on display for adoption, and I realized she was greatly dismayed.

"I'll get you out of here," I whispered.

Maggie was exactly the sort of cat I'd been advised to get to keep Ginger company. In fact, they have many characteristics in common.

I told Ginger that every day for two weeks, as he walked around the house grumbling, trying to avoid the newcomer. He hissed at her, from a safe distance, and she hissed back a time or two, but there was no outright violence. Sometimes Maggie followed Ginger down the hall, speaking in her high, girly voice, apparently asking if he would like to play. He made it clear he wouldn't.

I spent a lot of time singing Bette Midler's "You've Got to Have Friends," quoting Rodney King's "Can't we all just get along?" and providing general self-esteem counseling for my cats.

I kept them separated at night for ten days, but one morning when I opened the door to "her" bedroom, she darted out and into my room. There, she jumped on the bed just opposite from where Ginger lay, still sleeping. She squeaked out a message of some sort. His head jerked up, he staggered part way to his feet and he began to whine—not unlike my behavior when I first started sleeping with cats.

Now, I'm happy to report, they play together, eat together, nap together—and take turns waking me in the middle of the night.

March 15, 1997

Whale Watching

The woman's voice carried throughout the hotel lobby, even to the far reaches where I sat struggling with a jigsaw puzzle.

"I've just seen something I have never seen before," she said. "I've just seen something incredible!"

Fin whales. Fin whales, which grow up to eighty feet long and weigh sixty to seventy tons, second in size only to the mighty blue whale, which is the largest creature ever to live on Earth. Fin whales swimming, diving, feeding. That's what she was talking about, recounting her morning's adventure to the woman at the whale-watch registration desk.

I didn't look up from my puzzle, but I smiled. All over North America, people pay their money and get on boats, never quite believing that they will see whales in the wild. Usually, they do, and the powerful emotion reflected in that woman's voice is what leads them back to the boats again and again.

At the time, I was in the lobby of the Hotel Tadoussac on the St. Lawrence Seaway in Canada, passing time until the shuttle bus departed for the pier, where I had reservations for the afternoon whale watch. I had no doubt that I would see whales. I'd seen a dozen the day before, and I knew I would see them again.

The trip to Tadoussac in August marked my fifteenth year of whale watching. On September 25, 1982, I paid twenty-three dollars to board a boat in Barnstable, Massachusetts, hoping with all my being that I might actually see whales. The first whale of the day was a fin whale about the same size as our boat. The whale came toward us, dived and swam under the boat. It was gone before I could comprehend what I had seen. But there were more whales that day—dozens of hump-backs feeding and diving, one so close to the boat that I was baptized by the spray from its spout.

That day changed my life, bringing me to a profound regard for these magnificent creatures that have lived in the world's oceans for fifty million years.

All this came about because I read an article in July of 1982 in *The New York Times* about a whale-watch trip off Cape Cod. A photograph of a whale leaping out of the water accompanied the article. I stared at that photo for a long time, and decided that this was something I needed to see for myself. I headed for the library so I would know what I was looking at in case I ever saw a whale.

What an odd passion for someone who grew up here on the banks of the Mississippi River. Yet for fifteen years, I have set out in boats large and small to spend time in the company of blue whales, fin whales, right whales, humpbacks, gray whales, orcas, minkes and belugas.

In Alaska's Prince William Sound, the captain slowed to idle speed when a humpback whale approached our ferry. The whale stayed alongside for forty-five minutes, leaping completely out of the water dozens of times, slapping its fifteen-foot-long flipper on the water's surface repeatedly, sticking its ten-foot-wide scalloped tail up out of the water with every deep dive.

While drifting among whales and icebergs at dawn in a motorized Zodiac raft in Trinity Bay, we happened upon a frisky adolescent humpback, measuring about thirty-five feet long and weighing about a ton per foot. The animal draped its tail across the bow of our little rubber boat and gave us a hearty shove.

Relaxing on the back deck of a whale-watch boat out of

Monterey, California, I was startled to hear what sounded like a building exploding. I looked portside just in time to see the tower of vapor from a blue whale's spout. I watched the animal glide through the water and then disappear. On that same trip, investigating a patch of rough water up ahead, we found about a dozen frolicking orcas.

In San Ignacio Lagoon, off Baja California in Mexico, I watched a gray whale roll its big blue eye to observe me as I stroked her massive head. Another day out on the lagoon, I found myself with a ringside seat, watching a veritable flurry of fins and flukes as three gray whales courted.

Off Bar Harbor, Maine, I saw fish flying above the water's surface moments before I saw the cause of their distress: a seventy-two-foot-long fin whale that lunged halfway out of the water, mouth agape, to enjoy a good meal.

I spent an afternoon sitting in a boat off Peninsula Valdes in Argentina, listening to a female right whale softly snoring as her month-old offspring played beside her. Repeatedly, the baby lifted its head out of the water for a closer look at those of us on the boat.

I've also watched whales off British Columbia, in Hawaiian waters, off the coast of San Diego and just yards from the Oregon shore. In celebration of my fifteen years of watching whales, I invite you to consider spending a day on a tour boat, fully confident that you will indeed see what you came to see—and something incredible, at that.

September 27, 1997

Bachelor Party

No luck with the personals ads? Looking for a handsome bachelor? Midtown resident suit you just fine?

Meet Leo, Mshindi, Juma and Rafiki, all Western lowland gorillas living in a bachelor group at the St. Louis Zoo. In the wild, when young male gorillas leave their mothers, they tend to join a bachelor group for a few years before pursuing a mate. In 1987, Zoo officials set up such a group here, the first in the country.

Last month, the American Zoo and Aquarium Association honored the St. Louis Zoo with an award for the formation and long-term maintenance of the all-male group, which has included seven animals in the past eleven years.

"This award means a great deal to all of us," said Bob Merz, a primate keeper who routinely wins big toothy smiles from Leo, the eldest of the animals.

Leo, twenty, is a silverback, a mature male and the king of the hill among the males in the gorilla yard. One recent afternoon, Leo, who weighs 357 pounds, was stretched out on his back near a rock, idly scratching whatever itched and quietly watching the visitors peering down from above.

"All he needs is a remote and a beer, and he'd look just like my husband," said a Zoo visitor observing Leo.

Lowland gorillas come from western and central Africa. At the Zoo, the animals are fed fruit, vegetables and two kinds of nutritious chow. Zoo volunteers help keepers carry out an enrichment program that keeps the gorillas entertained.

As the only member of the original bachelor group, Leo has what Merz described as "a calming influence" on the group.

"He's calm, he's confident, and he doesn't challenge anyone. Leo is a very nice guy."

Mshindi, which means "winner" in Swahili, was born here in October of 1987, when the Cardinals were in the World Series. Merz said Mshindi is a high-spirited animal, somewhat skittish, and he plays rough. Perhaps eager to salvage his reputation, the 257-pound Mshindi sat quietly playing with a rope in the yard throughout my recent visit. Juma, Mshindi's ten-year-old brother, was sacked out under a rock overhang. Juma, who weighs 269 pounds, is calmer than Mshindi, and "a confident individual," said Merz. He added that Juma probably learned his demeanor from the late Fred, his and Mshindi's father.

Rafiki, a 372-pound fifteen-year-old, joins the other bachelors from time to time in the outdoor yard, and sometimes he is on display indoors. Rafiki came to the Zoo in 1991, and immediately took on the role of peacemaker. The other gorillas stayed away from Leo, but Rafiki sought Leo out and often played quietly with him. More recently, in his rowdy teen years, Rafiki teamed up with Jabari, a 388-pound, fourteen-year-old male, to harass Leo.

"When the testosterone kicks in between the ages of eleven and fifteen, male gorillas are very much like male humans of the same age," said Merz. "They get rambunctious, a little wild, full of pent-up energy, and they'll stand up to anyone."

In awkward social situations, gorillas, especially males, rely on threats, Merz said. "They will beat on their chests, roll around with each other, teeth flashing and hair standing on end. They'll even pull up grass and throw it at one another. Usually, all this commotion results only in small wounds, though males can inflict serious damage if they want to."

After a few rowdy incidents, Zoo officials decided to

place Rafiki in the indoor display with Nne, a ten-year-old, 164-pound female gorilla, and Kivu, who is almost twenty and weighs 178 pounds. Kivu is the mother of Mshindi and Juma. Zoo officials moved the two males into the outdoor display when they "started getting punky with their mother," said Merz, just another indication of puberty.

At first, Rafiki was fine with the females, interacting in positive ways through wires separating their displays. But Merz said that shortly after Rafiki was moved into the display, he started "roughing up" Kivu. Because Bachelor No. 1 didn't work out with the females, Zoo officials then introduced Jabari to Kivu and Nne.

At first, everything was great. Then, after spending a night in the same enclosure, Jabari and Nne began screaming at each other and tussling, so Jabari went back to his indoor bachelor pad.

"Introductions among primates always take a long time. Most likely, we'll wait awhile and then put Jabari back in with the females. This is all a transition period, an ongoing process, and it just takes awhile. Sometimes, there are these social difficulties," said Merz.

"And sometimes, it's a soap opera."

October 10, 1998

SATURDAY MORNING MUSINGS

Friends at the paper who want only the best for me—and there are some—have said for years that I needed to get my column switched to a different day, a "more important" day than Saturday. I routinely rejected this advice, even though it was well meant, because I knew something these friends at the paper did not know.

I knew, because readers repeatedly had told me, that Saturday was the only day most people have time to linger over the column with a second cup of coffee.

"It's my private time, and I choose to spend it with you," said one. Another woman said reading the column every Saturday was like a little visit with me, and she would never be able to make time on a Tuesday or Thursday. The best compliment of all was when a reader said she had come to believe that she and I were friends, because she's there with me every Saturday morning.

"I feel that I know you from your writing," she said.

"You do," I replied. And I meant it.

Thank you for joining me every Saturday morning, and thank you for being my friend.

Answering Machines

Don't call me; I'll call you.

If you do call me, I won't answer.

I never intended to quit answering the telephone. Time was, I'd run from wherever to catch the phone before it stopped ringing. No matter where I was—in the basement, in the yard, in the tub—I'd jump to attention at the first ring and race to the phone.

I can't remember why.

Now, I simply don't answer the telephone.

Somewhere along the line—probably when manufacturers started putting "off" buttons on the bottom of telephones—I started switching off the phone so I can sleep as late as I like without being interrupted.

Then I decided I wanted to eat meals when the food was hot, not when the random caller who has interrupted the meal is finished talking. There is no point, I decided, in answering the phone in the middle of a television program I especially want to see.

Answering the phone on the day of a big party is always a big mistake. After all, if I'll be spending the evening with my friends, why chat with them during the day when I needed to be cleaning the house or fixing the food? Surely they can figure out what to wear and how to get to my place without talking to me.

And I never, never answer the phone when I'm running out the door.

I grew up believing "If it's important, they'll call back."

I also grew up believing that everything plastic breaks, so I was adamantly opposed to answering machines. I wasn't just opposed. I was disdainful.

Who, I asked everybody I knew, is so important that they have to have an answering machine?

Everybody I know, apparently.

Early on, I hung up every time a machine answered. Then I found out that people who own machines use them to screen calls, and that if I identify myself and beg the people I had called to pick up the phone, often they do.

However, should our conversation be interrupted by a loud crackling sound that signals a call waiting on my friend's line, I hang up. Who is so important—besides Jerry Berger—that they need two phone lines?

Then the day came that an answering machine was a necessity in my house, for business purposes.

(Never say "never," a wise woman once intoned. The discussion at the time was in regard to living in Oklahoma. But I digress.)

I bought one. I dutifully recorded a speedy, uncute greeting. I sat back waiting for the machine to earn its keep.

At first, if I was home when the phone rang, and if I was in the mood to talk, I answered the phone in person, even though my machine was standing by.

One day, I realized that I don't ever have to answer the phone again.

Not that I would ever stoop to screening my calls. I simply don't answer any of them. A certain percentage of phone calls, like a certain percentage of mail, is just junk anyway. Sales calls. Product survey calls. Aluminum siding. Who cares if I miss those?

My boss calls a lot, but I figure he needs to learn to put out the paper without my help. My son calls periodically to check in, but he would prefer not to answer any questions even when we talk in person.

I always return business calls. And when my friends call, of course I call them back.

Now, I am considering changing the recording on my answering machine. I can't take credit for this message. I read it several years ago in Nicole Hollander's delightful comic strip "Sylvia."

If I recall correctly, it was a one-panel strip. Sylvia's cats are listening in as this message plays for a caller:

"No one is home to take your call right now. At the sound of the beep, hang up."

July 10, 1993

Worrisome Lasagna

Lasagna—and I say this with all due modesty, which is not very much because the fame is deserved—is my specialty. For nearly three decades, friends have flocked to my house for my lasagna. Then they have promptly plopped down on the couch for a little rest, so sated were they.

(My margaritas have had a similar effect on guests, but for entirely different reasons.)

How good is this lasagna? It's so good that I won't eat lasagna in restaurants anymore, as I know I'll be disappointed. It's so good that people call me and say, "How about having me over for lasagna?" It's so good that one friend recently asked me to teach him to make it.

I dug out the original recipe from *The Better Homes and Gardens New Cook Book*, published in 1968. Over the years, I've personalized the directions, putting in three times as much garlic, twice as many tomatoes and a tad more cheese.

My most secret ingredient is this: I worry.

Throughout the cooking process, I fret over each step as though I were making the recipe for the first time. I well remember how Tita's moods affected her cooking in Laura Esquivel's *Like Water for Chocolate*, and I'm convinced that my lasagna is outstanding because I care so deeply.

Here is the recipe, complete with directions on the proper attitude.

WORRISOME LASAGNA

1 pound Italian sausage
3 cloves garlic, minced
1 tablespoon whole basil
2 (14-ounce) cans tomatoes
3 (6-ounce) cans tomato paste
1/2 cup of dry red wine (optional)
10 ounces lasagna noodles
2 eggs
2 (15-ounce) containers Ricotta cheese
1/2 cup fresh grated Parmesan cheese
2 tablespoons parsley flakes
1/2 teaspoon pepper
1 pound mozzarella cheese, sliced thin
Preheat oven to 375 degrees.

In a large frying pan, brown meat slowly while you regret that sausage isn't good for you. Acknowledge that it gives the lasagna a much better flavor than ground beef. Spoon off excess fat.

Add garlic, basil (crush it between your palms to release the flavor), tomatoes and tomato paste. If you've bought unpeeled whole tomatoes, worry that they'll lie in the sauce in big clumps. If you've bought peeled and diced tomatoes, fret that they won't add enough heft. Simmer uncovered (the sauce, not you) for 30 minutes.

If you're in the mood and you have it on hand, add the wine and simmer 10 minutes more. Remove from heat.

In a big pot, cook noodles in boiling salted water until

tender. The challenge here is avoiding overcooked noodles. Packaged lasagna noodles always taste a little overcooked. Fresh lasagna noodles sometimes seem to cook even before they are immersed in the boiling water. It's a dilemma. Drain and rinse the noodles, hoping for the best.

In a large mixing bowl, beat eggs. Stir in Ricotta, Parmesan, parsley flakes and pepper. Ask yourself: Will this be enough cheese mixture? Will it be too much? Oh, dear!

Layer half the noodles in a 13-by-9-by-2-inch baking dish, overlapping each one by about half. Tear two or three noodles to fit that empty space at the end of the dish. With a spatula, evenly spread half the Ricotta mixture over the noodles. It's scary; take your time. Place half the mozzarella slices over the Ricotta mixture. The cheese slices never really fit right, so tear them into strips to fill in where needed. Spread on half the meat sauce. Worry that you'll miscalculate what constitutes half, because sometimes the sauce rearranges itself in the pan.

Repeat the previous paragraph. You'll be running out of everything, and it's too late if you've divided wrong. Also, expect to have a few noodles left over. Don't try to think of uses for them; throw them down the disposal and get on with your day.

Bake lasagna about 30 to 40 minutes. If the lasagna bubbles over in the oven, you'll have to clean it up. Are you prepared for that? Let stand 10 minutes before serving.

Serves 8 to 10, or so the cookbook says, but people always want second helpings, so don't count on serving that many. Maybe you should have made two pans.

Just kidding! And don't worry—everybody will love the lasagna.

March 2, 1996

Shoes, Count 'em, Shoes

Time for a personal question: How many pairs of shoes do you own?

In Linda O'Keeffe's *Shoes: A Celebration of Pumps, Sandals, Slippers & More*, I read that the average American woman has thirty pairs.

"You have lots more than that," said my friend, Edward.

I denied it. He headed down the hall to count my shoes, betting me a box of ice cream sandwiches that I own more than thirty pairs. He rummaged through my sandals, my flats, my boots. He found my sneakers and my purple Chinese Mary Janes. He looked in the boxes that hold my grown-up lady shoes, which most of the world has never seen on my feet.

Edward found twenty-seven pairs of shoes, not counting my beloved plush Grimmy slippers. I announced that instead of a crummy box of ice cream sandwiches, I wanted a pint of Jamoca almond fudge ice cream.

Edward remained calm, convinced that he had won the bet.

"I'm sure you have more shoes. You're hiding them," he said.

Again, I denied the charge. Grinning, Edward left. I went into the Tea Party Room to look for a book. There, I saw my pewter flats—uncounted—resting in the magazine rack. Oops! Later, in the basement, I noticed my silver high-heeled dancing slippers tucked into an empty champagne bucket, still waiting for the next dance. That pushed the tally up to twenty-nine.

I marched right to the telephone and called a shoe store I had accidentally visited the day before. I asked the sales clerk to set aside a pair of gold sandals that I had rejected as unnecessary. Suddenly, I needed them. If I'm going to lose a bet, I want to be well-shod.

Why do we have so many shoes? After all, we can only wear two at a time. In her splendid little book on shoes, O'Keeffe writes: "It's the thrill of slipping into a new shoe and a new persona that piques desire."

O'Keeffe continues: "The indefinable allure of a new shoe unlocks rich private fantasies. We fall for a fabulous shoe at first glance, seduced by the tilt of a heel or the sensuous line of an arch. The whimsy of a flirtatious bow, the nearly edible appeal of a decorative frosting of beads or swirls of embroidery all add up to fatal attraction."

Apparently, true collectors don't stop with that thirtieth pair, but own as many as 500. If you have that many shoes—and you're not selling retail or at a wholesale outlet—write and tell me about your collection. Also, if you have a spectacular story about any single pair of shoes, I'd like to hear that, too. Please don't call, but send notes to me at the *St. Louis Post-Dispatch*.

Collecting shoes is one thing. A friend collects knit pants. Last time I visited her, she proudly showed me stacked bins full of knit pants, sorted by color and pattern. Are you sitting down? She has seventy-two pairs. Sixteen of them are navy blue!

She admits she didn't set out to collect knit pants. (Well, who would?) But when she gave up wearing little wool dresses, she slipped into something more comfortable—knit pants— and now she has a jillion. OK, seventy-two. This woman just can't say no.

"So I'm promiscuous when it comes to clothes," she said. "So?"

I suggested that she share some of her collection with the less fortunate. She said she does that often, adding, "I gave nearly all my purses to the Veterans."

Rather than contemplate how many veterans actually carry

purses, I prefer to move on and tell you about a recent health scare. We're talking mental health. Last week, I suffered an attack of Gracious Living.

I know why. My friends Beth and Rick just bought a new house. My friend Suzy, just bought a new house. My friend Gail just redecorated. Frankly, in comparison to all these fresh starts, my house seemed stale.

I rearranged a couple of pictures on the walls. I moved all the furniture on the east wall of my home office to the west wall. I bought some inexpensive beaded curtains to up the exotic quotient of my bedroom. Still, something was missing— Flowers!

Never in my life have I been in one of those stores that sells dried and silk flowers. Last week, I was in such a store three times. I went in twice to look at a lovely basket of silk sunflowers, and left it there because I suspected it was too big for the space I had in mind. The third time, I took along a tape measure, confirmed that it was indeed too large—and bought it anyway.

At home, I put the basket in the corner where I had imagined it would look best. It stuck out into the hall. I tried it on the coffee table. There was no room for the remote, much less a glass of Pepsi. I moved it to a small round table between the sofa and the loveseat. Silk fronds dangled over onto both couches.

This particular basket of silk sunflowers was not just a little too big. It was immense. I returned it to the store, and am feeling much better now. Gracious or un.

April 12, 1997

The Fantasticks

As I sat in the posh new theater at St. Louis University High School earlier this month, watching the Dauphin Players strut their stuff in Tom Jones' and Harvey Schmidt's musical *The Fantasticks*, I was present in the moment, happy to be there with my longtime friends Susan Cuddihee and her brother, Bob Overkamp.

But in the course of the evening, as I watched the young actors, sometimes their faces and voices blurred slightly, and momentarily changed into those of other young actors, Dauphin Players who performed in *The Fantasticks* at St. Louis University High School in December of 1965.

I was there thirty-two years ago when drama teacher Joe Schulte-now in his fortieth year of teaching at SLUH-presented the first high school production of *The Fantasticks* in the United States.

More to the point, I was there with Susan and Bob. At the time, Susan and I were seniors at Webster Groves High School and Bob was a junior at SLUH, where he now works as a computer specialist.

The Fantasticks has remained important to the three of us, and we've each made a point of seeing it whenever possible.

That first production, held in the old auditorium at SLUH, featured Jim Byrnes as Henry, David Deutch as El Gallo and Tom Jasorka as Mortimer. Byrnes, now living in Vancouver, found fame as a blues singer and a television actor in "Wiseguy" and "Highlander." Jasorka's first play was just produced in Fort Collins, Colorado. As for the El Gallo who lives forever in my heart, well, Schulte said he has lost track of Deutch.

But what they did after high school, even who they are

now, matters less to me than the phenomenal impression these talented young men made as characters in this most charming, thought-provoking musical.

For those of you who don't know *The Fantasticks*, it is a love story about a girl, a boy, their parents and a wall built to bring together what may otherwise have been kept apart. Luisa, the teen-age girl, speaks aloud her most urgent prayer: "Please, God, please—don't let me be normal!" Matt, the boy, compares Luisa to Polaris (the one trustworthy star), to September, to the microscopic inside of a leaf.

The boy's father is a retired Navy man who takes great pride in his garden. The girl's father (or mother, in some contemporary versions) is a button maker who grows kumquats. El Gallo serves as the narrator, a rogue and a sometime romantic interest for Luisa after Matt leaves to make his way in the world. Henry and Mortimer are traveling actors who take roles where they find them, comforted by the knowledge that "there are no small actors—only small parts." Henry's specialty is Shakespeare; Mortimer dies. The remaining character in the play is a mute, who plays the wall, provides the rain and otherwise assists throughout.

The most important theme that runs through the play, spoken by El Gallo, is this: "There is a curious paradox that no one can explain. Who understands the secret of the reaping of the grain? Who understands why Spring is born out of Winter's laboring pain? Or why we all must die a bit before we grow again."

The Fantasticks opened on May 3, 1960, at the Sullivan Street Playhouse in New York. Jerry Orbach, the voice of Lumiere in *Beauty and The Beast* and a regular on "Law & Order," was the original El Gallo. Among the actors who have performed in the show are Anna Maria Alberghetti, Richard Chamberlain, Elliott Gould, Edward Everett Horton, Bert Lahr, Liza

Minnelli, F. Murray Abraham and Glenn Close. The longest running show in the history of American theater, *The Fantasticks* still can be seen at the Sullivan Street Playhouse.

Alas, I have yet to see the show in New York, but I've seen *The Fantasticks* at least two dozen times, including amateur and professional productions. Susan has lost count. Bob didn't offer a firm number either, but he's probably seen it more often than any of us.

When Bob played Hucklebee, the boy's father, in a production at the University of Michigan early in 1968, Susan and I boarded a Greyhound bus and made the grueling trip—perhaps the most trouble we've ever gone to just to see a play.

It was no trouble to prepare the salad, lasagna and apple pie that I made for our dinner before the play on December 6. It was a little trouble to sing "Happy Birthday" to Susan, as I'm no singer, but Bob helped, and the song certainly was in order, as we were celebrating Susan's birthday. Soon after dinner, we headed for the theater at SLUH. The house lights went down, the overture got us in the mood and then Greg Etling, as El Gallo, stepped forward and began to sing "Try to Remember."

Oh, I remember. I remember.

December 20, 1997

Missed the Mark

Sometimes, you please everybody, saying just what they want to hear. Other days, you miss the mark. Such is the lot of a public speaker.

I had one of those "miss the mark" days not too long ago when I spoke to fourth- and fifth-graders at a local elementary school. They were celebrating Author Day, and as the author of four children's nature books, I was the guest speaker.

My story about how I got into this line of work—by accident, actually—wasn't the problem. I don't think any of them were disappointed in the tales I told about the struggles and triumphs I experienced while writing the books. And I know that many of the students like the finished product, as they brought copies for me to autograph.

No, I didn't miss the mark on those points.

The question period, when I asked the students to tell me what they wanted to know, is where the morning turned dicey. Oh, I answered every question earnestly, as each question was asked just that way. But later, driving away from the school, I realized that my answers to some of the questions fell far short of what the students had hoped to hear.

They liked it when I answered the question about a character in one book named after their teacher. They laughed when I explained how an entire reindeer came to be found in the stomach of a dead shark. They shrieked with glee when I responded that one of my all-time favorite books is *Mr. Popper's Penguins*, clearly a favorite among the students as well.

No, it was my answers to the personal questions that disappointed.

Q. Where do you live?

A. Shrewsbury.

Q. What kind of car do you drive?

A. An Oldsmobile.

Q. How much money did you make on these books?

A. Very little, and I had to give part of it to my literary agent and part of it to the government.

Q. Do you make your living writing books?

A. No, I make my living working for the *Post-Dispatch*. I spend what I earn from the books on vacations to study more animals so I can write more books.

See what's happening here? None of my answers were

quite what the students had expected.

Clearly, they had assumed that I live in Ladue, drive a Lamborghini, have more money than Bill Gates and can live on Easy Street for the rest of my life because I'm an author.

I should have seen this coming when the first child that I called on asked me my age. I could tell from the expression on his face when I told him that he was shocked that someone as old as I am could have driven myself to the school, much less written books in my dotage.

Next, I disappointed a little boy who wondered aloud if my husband approved of my work. I responded that I don't have a husband, haven't had one for years, but that I was reasonably certain that the man I was once married to thinks that my writing books is a fine idea.

Once my answers had established that I failed to live up to their preconceived notions about authors, the students went back to questions about sharks, manatees, dolphins and beavers. Then, this:

Q. Does it make you mad that you have to give money to your agent?

A. No, I'm happy that she has helped me get my books published, so I'm happy to share my earnings.

Q. Why do you give some of your money to the government?

A. What a good question! I give money to the government because in this country, if you earn a living, the government expects you to pay taxes. They take your money and build highways and schools, which are a good idea, and nuclear weapons, which are not. But whether or not I want to, I have to pay. Everybody does.

Then, it was back to the gory stuff.

Q. Did that reindeer in the shark's stomach have teeth marks on it?

A. I can't say for sure, but I suspect so.

I did OK on the question about which of my books is my favorite—it's *Manatees For Kids*, because I love those big, graceful animals that spend their days floating serenely and gently nibbling on water lilies.

Because the animals are gentle, many scientists have believed that they also are dumb, I said, and isn't it a shame that peaceful creatures are thought to be stupid? A severely endangered species, manatees are routinely run over by speed boats in Florida, and I reported that some of the wounded manatees being cared for at animal sanctuaries have been trained to perform complex behaviors, so maybe they aren't so dumb after all.

The students also seemed interested when I told them that the legend of the mermaid is supposedly based on ancient sailors' sightings of manatees.

Anyway, my morning with the students taught me something I hadn't known but should have guessed—that success, in the minds of youngsters, equals wealth.

On behalf of the many hardly-famous-at-all and nowhere-near-rich authors, I apologize.

May 16, 1998

A Born-Again Baseball Fan

Welcome to my new baseball trivia call-in show. You're on the air.

Hello?

Hello—what is your question?

Am I on the air?

Yes, you are. Go ahead with your question.

I was wondering how the Cardinals feel about their visible

panty lines.

I beg your pardon?

You know, just below mid-thigh on most of the Cardinals, you can see a line where the special "boxer briefs" they wear ends. How do they feel about it?

I'll have to check with Rick or Mike or Bernie and get back to you on that. Thanks for calling.

Welcome to my new baseball trivia call-in show. You're on the air.

Is that you, Pat?

Yes, it's me. Did you have a question?

Yes. Am I on the air?

You are indeed—ask away.

What is a "ribbie"?

Are you referring to some kind of pork sandwich at McDonald's?

No, it's something Mike Shannon says from time to time. A "ribbie."

Oh—that's Runs Batted In, which used to be known as "RBIs." Once in awhile, Shannon calls them "ribbies."

Welcome to my new baseball trivia call-in show. Go ahead please, you're on the air.

Hello?

Hello. What's your question?

Hey, Pat I've known you a couple of years, and I've been under the impression that you didn't think much of sports. But I happen to know you're gathering at the water cooler at work to talk baseball. What's up?

Thanks for your call, but we're all out of time on this show. Check my column in the Saturday *St. Louis Post-Dispatch* for your answer. Look here, too, for an acknowledgment to my former colleague Kevin Horrigan for a great way to start a column.

What can I tell you? I'm a born-again Cardinals fan.

This all started last summer, with Mark McGwire. I like what I know of him, and I like what he's done for baseball. That's all—a respect for the man brought me back to baseball, which was an important part of my past.

When transistor radios first came along, one of the best things about them was you could carry your radio wherever you wanted and listen to the ball game, instead of sitting inside in one place. My Dad was a big Cardinals fan, as was my grandfather. And so was I, all through the '60s. On weekends, I'd gather up my radio and my sunscreen and lie on a lounge chair in the backyard, listening to Harry Caray announce the games.

Other weekends, I'd sit out back with Daddy while he barbecued, and we'd tune in KMOX. At the beginning of the game, Daddy would crank the grate on the Weber kettle up to its highest point. Mid-game, Mom would stick her head out the back door and ask, "How's that chicken doing? How much longer?"

"Bonnie," Daddy would say, "we're only in the bottom of the sixth. This chicken has three innings to go."

On doubleheader days, we didn't eat until really late.

So I grew up listening to baseball, caring about the players, knowing how the game was played. I even read the sports stories in the paper after the game, to relive the excitement— or disappointment. Like everybody else my age, I have a ball autographed by Stan Musial, Ken Boyer, Lindy McDaniel and Joe Cunningham.

Then, everything changed. I went off to college. I got married. I had a child. I went back to work when my son was five. The years just melted away. I knew that the Cardinals still played, of course, but I didn't know anything about them. I'd lost track, lost interest.

Then, last year I went to a ball game and sat in one of the fancy field boxes. Surprisingly, I found myself paying attention to the game, and I remembered much more than I would have imagined. When McGwire came up to bat, a wave of excitement rippled through the crowd, and it got to me, too. I loved being there, and I loved watching him, and I paid attention to Cardinals baseball the rest of the season.

This year, it's different. I'm still a McGwire fan, but the game itself and the other players matter, too. I watch or listen to the games when I can, and I always read the report in the paper the next day. I even bought myself a Cardinals T-shirt and some red shorts. Hey—I'm back with baseball, and I'm ready!

May 15, 1999

Bureaucrats Unlimited

Standing behind a counter all day telling people they failed to bring everything they need must be a thankless job. Yet many an office in town is staffed with workers willing to do just that.

You've been there. We've all been there. At long last, you reach the front of the line, clutching half a dozen Official Papers, only to be told by the clerk at your neighborhood license bureau that you don't have everything you need.

Maybe a support group is in order. Certainly, this experience lowers self-esteem. First of all, this is a public humiliation. No clerk ever whispers about your failure. Suddenly, you feel like you're back in fourth grade, when you handed in only half your math homework—the half you understood.

Excuses do not sway the clerks at the license bureaus. "I don't remember the car dealer telling me I would need that," you say, jutting out your chin to keep it from quivering at your inadequacy.

"Well, if I were you, I'd call that dealer," is the response. Then: "Next person, please." You've been dismissed.

Sometimes, money will sway the clerks. "Wait—please give me another chance," you say. "I paid my personal property tax, even if I didn't bring the receipt. The state must have a record of it. Can't you just look it up on the computer?"

You learn that for three dollars, the clerk can fax a request to Jefferson City for a copy of your personal property tax receipt. Three dollars is nothing compared to the aggravation of driving back home, shuffling through a folder of Official Papers and driving back. "I'll pay it," you say.

The clerk jots down some notes and slips the paper into the fax machine. Nothing happens. She tries again. Nothing. She calls Jefferson City. The line is busy. The people behind you who previously were grumbling about the long wait now make personal remarks about you. The clerk dials the number again. This time, the line is free. Then you hear her say in a concerned voice, "The fax machine is broken?"

So you drive home and get the piece of paper, the only piece of paper in the universe that the clerk needs to see so the state will graciously accept the absurd amount of tax you owe on your new car. Perhaps Missourians should all move to Illinois, where they don't play this particular game.

You return to the license bureau, relatively calm and eager to resume your usually pleasant mood. This time, you won't be turned away. Ha!—that's what you think.

You join the line once again. When it's your turn, a different clerk waits on you. She shuffles through your Official Papers. A creature of habit, she intones, "You don't have everything you need. I don't see an inspection statement here." For a moment, you panic. Then you realize the inspection statement is on the bottom of the pile and that the clerk has overlooked it. Is it your imagination, or is she mildly irritated that you do, indeed, have every single piece of paper required? Wisely, you remain silent.

Your excitement builds. After just two trips and a minor hitch, this finally is working out. This errand you dreaded for days is almost over, this tedious mission almost accomplished. The clerk calculates the amount of tax you owe. You shudder when you hear the number, but write out the check. You start to reclaim your Official Papers, more than ready to exhale a sigh of relief. Then the clerk says, "I can't take this check."

Frustration, long stifled, boils up. You ask why she cannot accept the check. She replies that it looks like a check issued from a credit card company and that she can't take those checks. You speak up, spitting out each word with great deliberation: "This is not a credit card check. This check is from a money market account. It has the name of the bank on it and it has my name and address on it. This check has nothing to do with a credit card company."

You pause for breath and quickly realize you will lose the advantage if you stop talking. "Furthermore," you add in a semi-threatening tone, "this is the only account that I have with any money, so if you want to collect the tax on the car, you will accept this check."

The people in line behind you snicker. The clerk remains unconvinced. She waves your check at her boss. "I can't take this check, right?" she asks, trying to prejudice him against the innocent piece of paper. He stares at the check. He sees your name on the check and points to it.

"Is that her?" he asks the clerk. "If that's her, you can take it."

This woman who spends forty hours a week telling people they failed to bring everything they need looks at her boss. She looks at the check. She looks at me. The wind shifts. In defeat, she says, "I guess so." With much ceremony, she bundles up the Official Papers that she gets to keep, including the check, and calls for the next person to approach the counter. The glint in her eye lets you know that you got off easy, but don't expect any favors next time you show up without everything you need.

April 1, 2000

Fun at the Emissions Testing Station

Up for ninety minutes of drama? You'll laugh, you'll cry, you'll offer your kingdom for a horse as you watch performances depicting every emotion in the human repertoire, live and unrehearsed and now playing at a new "enhanced" emissions testing station in a neighborhood near you.

Maybe you've read about the new testing stations in this newspaper. Maybe your license plates are due for renewal and you got a colorful, tri-fold brochure in the mail about the testing stations. Or maybe you're ignoring the whole thing, hoping the whole thing will go away. That isn't going to happen. Like it or not, eventually you will end up in a line at one of the emissions stations. There you will hear loud music playing in other cars, you will see people run out of gas and patience at the same time, and you will smell more burning oil and exhaust fumes than the law ought to allow.

Be warned—there are no concession stands.

One morning last week, I decided to visit the emissions station near my house. I had no intention whatsoever of having the inspection performed just yet. I simply wanted information about estimated wait times at the various stations, and I needed to know whether the twenty-four-dollar fee, mentioned prominently in the brochure, had to be in cash. Supposedly, the answers to my questions were available by calling 888-748-4227, a hot line set up by the Gateway Clean Air Program, which is part of the Missouri Department of Natural Resources. For a week, I called that number whenever I had a minute. I never got through, so I figured I'd just pop over to the nearest station and see what was what.

Let's just say the stations don't encourage visits from people seeking information. I followed the winding route to the station, ending up in a parking lot in an industrial court. Just ahead, I saw a ticket machine, with cars lined up beyond it. Before I could decide whether to turn and park or move ahead and take a ticket, a car pulled up behind me with a driver who wanted me to get a move on. I drove toward the ticket machine, still thinking I had options.

Be warned—once you get in the lane that leads to the ticket machine, you're trapped. It's no different from changing your mind about riding the roller coaster once you've been locked into your seat. It's no different from deciding not to jump off the high dive once you've climbed up all fifty-four steps and three dozen people are behind you. It's no different from trying to park behind Blue Water Grill in Kirkwood and being funneled into the drive-through lane at Taco Bell, which is adjacent to the parking lot. Once you take that ticket, there is no turning back. At least in the drive-through lane at Taco Bell, a person could buy a Pepsi.

Just past the ticket machine, cars were lining up n five lanes that all led to the testing stations. A sign said that Lane One was only for four-wheel-drive vehicles. Because I believe what I read, I chose Lane Two, just in time to watch a zippy little four-cylinder car pull ahead of me in Lane One. "Harrumph," I thought. "He will just have to wait that much longer when he is turned away at the station," which was six or seven car lengths ahead.

That didn't happen. Cars of all sizes and drive capabilities were accepted in Lane One. That should have been my first clue that the other signs were just for fun, too, but I persisted in behaving like a model citizen. No fewer than five signs on the property repeat the three rules of the day. First, drivers are to remain in their vehicles. Inexplicably, drivers in cars all around me were opening their doors and getting out of their cars. Several young drivers, working for used car dealers this summer, all seemed to know one another from previous trips to the station. They car-hopped, laughing and talking with friends. Still other drivers got out to change shirts, store stuff in the trunk or go off in search of a concession stand.

The next rule prohibits drivers from turning off their car engines. Ha! Every person there clearly had been to Steak 'n' Shake, where everybody turns off their cars while waiting in the drive-through lane. They did the same thing here, even though no steakburgers or strawberry shakes awaited them at the end of the line.

The third rule is the most deceptive. The signs state that the fee for the test is twenty-four dollars. The signs also go on to mention that Visa, MasterCard or checks made out to G.P.A.C. are accepted. At least that answered one of my questions. Dutifully, remaining in my car and wasting gas with the engine running as I waited, I wrote a check for twenty-four dollars. It turns out the fee varies depending on how long you have to wait. I had to tear up that check and write another one for fourteen dollars. And don't think you can get tested for free. The lowest fee is four dollars, and that's after a two-hour wait.

Be warned—after you finally complete your emissions test, to get your license renewed you still have to get a safety inspection at your service station or car dealer. Then, and only then, can you go get in line at the license bureau. And that's another drama altogether.

June 17, 2000

About the Author

Patricia Corrigan, a native St. Louisan, is a reporter and columnist for the *St. Louis Post-Dispatch*.

Since January of 1992, her Saturday morning column has offered up interesting interviews, funny bits, heart-warming stories and controversial topics. Her subjects may be local, but her themes are universal, and she has repeatedly been praised for taking on "matters of the heart" not often found in the pages of today's newspapers.

She also is the author of *The Whale Watcher's Guide* (NorthWord Press, Third Edition) and six children's nature books from NorthWord Press: *Dolphins for Kids*, *Sharks for Kids*, *Manatees for Kids*, *Beavers for Kids*, *Our Wild World: Whales*, and *Our Wild World: Cougars* (Fall 2001). Her dessert cookbook, *Angels in the Kitchen*, is no longer in print. She has had articles published in such magazines as *Family Fun*, *Diversions*, *Cruise Travel*, *Radiance*, *Northwest Parks and Wildlife*, *Ms.*, and the defunct *BBW* and *Lear's*.

She has one son, a telecommunications engineer in northern California. She shares her home in St. Louis County with an orange cat and a tortoise cat. Someday, maybe she will own a convertible.